The

TRIUMPH
of
DISCOVERY

The TRIUMPH of DISCOVERY

Women Scientists Who Won the Nobel Prize

BY JOAN DASH

JULIAN MESSNER

JULIAN MESSNER and colophon are trademarks of Simon & Schuster, Inc.

Design by Virginia Pope-Boehling

Manufactured in the United States of America.
Lib. ed. 10 9 8 7 6 5 4 3 2 1
Paper ed. 10 9 8 7 6 5 4 3 2 1
Library of Congress Cataloging-in-Publication Data

Dash, Joan.
    The Triumph of Discovery: Women Scientists Who Won the Nobel Prize by Joan
    Dash.
        p.   cm.
    Includes index.
    Summary: Examines the lives of Barbara McClintock, Maria Mayer, Rosalyn
Yalow, and Rita Levi-Montalcini, women scientists who won the Nobel Prize
against extraordinary odds, in different fields and under different circumstances.
        1. McClintock, Barbara, 1902–   —Juvenile literature.   2. Mayer, Maria Goeppert,
1906–1972—Juvenile literature.   3. Yalow, Rosalyn S. (Rosalyn Sussman), 1921–
—Juvenile literature.   4. Levi-Montalcini, Rita—Juvenile literature.   5. Women
medical scientists—Biography—Juvenile literature.   6. Women scientists—
Biography—Juvenile literature.   7. Nobel prizes—Juvenile literature.   8. Medical
scientists—Biography—Juvenile literature.   9. Scientists—Biography—Juvenile
literature.   [1. McClintock, Barbara, 1902–   . 2. Mayer, Maria Goeppert, 1906–
1972. 3. Yalow, Rosalyn S. (Rosalyn Sussman), 1921–   . 4. Levi-Montalcini,
Rita. 5. Women scientists. 6. Scientists. 7. Nobel prizes.]   I. Title.
R692.D36   1990
509.2′2—dc20
[B]
[920]   90-39308
                                                                              CIP
                                                                              AC

ISBN 0-671-69332-8 (lib. bdg.)
ISBN 0-671-69333-6 (pbk.)

CONTENTS

Since Nobel prizes were first awarded in 1901, nearly five hundred have been given in the sciences, ten of them to women. This means that on ten different occasions a woman was judged by her peers to be worthy of immortality, for Nobel Prizes have that effect.

These prizes are the only child of a shy, unhappy Swedish bachelor, Alfred Nobel, who invented dynamite and became one of the richest men in the world. Perhaps out of a sense of guilt, he left most of his fortune to a fund, the interest to be used as annual awards to those who had contributed the most to mankind during the preceding year. The will was written by hand on four crowded pages, even the margins densely covered in writing, and it all but denied the existence of Nobel's relatives, who were rich and powerful and likely to contest it.

There were other problems. How were the prizewinners to be chosen? How was the fund to be administered? The will had nothing to say on these matters. Another, more pressing question: could a will of that kind, properly witnessed, but written without a lawyer, and legally weak, stand up in court?

Almost one hundred years later, Nobel's will is still gloriously alive and doing what he intended—rewarding excellence. There are other international prizes, some even more lucrative, but the Nobel remains the most sought-after. It is the one that brings tears to the eyes of an unexpected winner, while those who think they should have won are sometimes haunted forever by the lack of this single elusive honor.

The annual announcement of prizewinners makes front-page headlines. Throughout the world, millions of people look forward to following the prize-giving ceremonies on radio or television. And in Sweden, where the prizes have always been given by the king or crown prince, Nobel Week is a festival of light in the long, dark, Northern winter.

Most of the laureates are scientists, but not all. Nobel decreed that the awards were to be given in five fields, Physics, Chemistry, Medicine or Physiology, Literature, and Peace; a sixth field, Economics, has since been added. The awarding institutions remain as Nobel listed them in his will. People call these institutions the Big Four, and there are still only four: in the sciences, the Academy of Science, and Sweden's leading hospital, the Karolinska; in Literature, the eighteen-member Swedish Academy; for the Peace prize, the Norwegian Nobel Committee.

Every year each of the Big Four invites suggestions from two to three thousand individuals, including university professors in Africa, scientists in Malaysia, and writers' organizations in the USSR. Former Nobelists are always asked for suggestions.

Then five-member committees from the Big Four retire behind closed doors for discussions leading to the final decision, a process that takes most of a year. What happens behind those doors remains utterly secret; it is a formal policy that nothing is to be revealed of the sometimes heated discussions that lead up to the decision, at least not until fifty years have passed, and the prizewinner in question is dead.

On a day in late October a door opens, someone comes out, cameras flash, and a statement is read announcing the prizewinners. The press responds with a barrage of questions: Was the choice unanimous? Why wasn't Professor X selected? Was Professor Y at least close? Silence is the only answer. No matter what choices were made, or what arguments were raised against them, nothing will be changed.

After the announcement to journalists come the telephone calls to the laureates themselves. In the case of American winners, these calls come very early in the morning, so most are wakened from sleep by the overseas operator. There are press conferences that morning, interviews, photographers, telegrams and flowers, and more phone calls from friends, and a sense of being besieged by fame.

Then the laureates and their families make the trip to Stockholm, where on December 10 the prizes are to be presented in the Concert Hall. All the new laureates rehearse the program that morning, everyone is told where to sit, stand, and walk. Later that day they return to the Concert Hall, the women in evening dress, the men in white tie and tails, either borrowed or rented. They enter the hall only after the audience of two thousand is already in place and the Swedish royal family seated in the front row. The women of the royal family wear jewels and tiaras, while the men wear their medals and ribbons.

As the laureates come in, the king rises to greet them—nowadays, King Karl Gustav XVI, who has inherited the role from his grandfather. For many of the laureates this is the most moving part of the ceremony, the king's standing up in their honor.

A gold medal weighing half a pound, and a large sum of money (tax-free for American winners) accompany each prize. When the ceremony is over, a banquet takes place in the Town Hall, to which each of the laureates and their family members are escorted by one of the royals.

On the final day of Nobel Week, laureates are awakened in their hotel rooms at six in the morning by young members of the hotel staff, all dressed in white robes; the girls wear wreaths on their heads, or crowns bearing burning white candles, in honor of a Swedish tradition paying homage to Lucia, the queen of light.

The fairy tale comes to an end. The laureates return home, where their lives will never again be the same. As Rosalyn Yalow, Nobel laureate in Medicine for 1977, has said, "a Nobel prizewinner can do no wrong." Sometimes the magic of the Nobel is almost too powerful. The physicist T.D. Lee, who won the prize in 1957 when in his early thirties, is said to have exclaimed, "My God! What happens now to the rest of my life? What comes after this?"

The four women scientists whose life stories follow are therefore members of a very small group—women—within a select group, the Nobel laureates. Whatever procedures were used to choose them, there was no affirmative action. Nobody said, "Let's have a woman this year." They were chosen because their fellow scientists saw their work as the best in its field. In some cases it was a single brilliant, illuminating theory that made possible new ways of thinking; in others, it was a life's work, but in every case it was judged to be the best.

So what these four accomplished they did against extraordinary odds. They had few if any role models, and during the first half of the century, when they built their careers, they were unwelcome in most graduate institutions.

They went into science out of a love of science—it was something they did for themselves, purely for the joy of it. When not at work they thought, breathed, and talked science; their friends were scientists; the two who married chose fellow scientists, believing no one else could truly understand them. They expected their children to become scientists as well, for no other life seemed to offer the same pleasures and rewards, which had nothing to do with money. One of the four worked for years without pay, and all were indifferent to money. Science itself was the reward, just as the act of making music is a musician's reward.

The four are Maria Mayer, Rosalyn Yalow, Barbara McClintock, and Rita Levi-Montalcini. And while their work made scientific history, their lives are essentially romantic ones—love affairs with science—for the goal of love is intimacy with the beloved, knowledge of the beloved. Like all proper love stories, these involve difficult roads, pitfalls, hairpin turns, as well as frustrations and rivalries and moments when all seems lost. Sometimes the happy endings come when least expected.

Maria Mayer

CHAPTER 1

MARIA GOEPPERT-MAYER:

1963 Nobel Prize for Physics

"THE WALTZ WITHIN THE NUCLEUS"

This is how Maria Mayer remembered the day of the bomb. She'd been walking on the beach in Nantucket with Joe and the children, having their first family vacation since the war began, when one of the neighbors came toward them at a run. As she caught up, the woman called out the news she'd heard on the radio, that an atomic bomb had been dropped on a place called Hiroshima.

Maria's first thought was, "How I wish it hadn't worked!" Then, with a rush of relief, she realized she'd be able to tell her husband everything now. And after that she noted the way the neighbor turned to Joe, saying, "Did you have anything to do with the atomic bomb, Professor Mayer?" Not to Maria—to Joe. It was a small detail that remained fixed in Maria's memory. Both were scientists. Both had been doing war work. Yet when the neighbor heard this astonishing news she naturally turned to Joe.

No, he said, he'd had nothing to do with it, knew nothing about it. After a while the woman left; the children were nudged and shoved till they walked on ahead, and then Maria started to talk, letting it all pour out, so fast, so compulsively, that her words ran together like water. She had a habit of speaking fast when excited; her voice was low to begin with, her German accent grew stronger when under tension, and she had so much to say, so much that had been stored up within her for three difficult years.

She saw the children from a distance. Peter, the younger, wanted to run back, but Marianne kept him from running. This was another memory of the day, the knowledge that she couldn't have spoken freely if the children were there. She would have to rehearse what she told them, would have to speak calmly, reassuringly. She had worked on the bomb project, her dearest friends, the people she most admired, had worked more intimately with it, and at the same time she had hoped it would never succeed.

Maria Goeppert-Mayer was born in 1906 in Kattowitz, a German city that is now Polish. Her parents were Dr. Friedrich Goeppert and his wife, Maria. Four years later the family moved to Göttingen, a little medieval town in central Germany, known throughout the Western world—especially among mathematicians—for its university. Dr. Goeppert was appointed professor of pediatrics at Göttingen, and Maria grew up there, an only child in a big, comfortable house, with servants, and the bustle of company, and beautiful dinner parties for which all the rooms were thrown open and filled with flowers. Göttingen in those days was a festive place, alive with students, busy with theater, opera, and concerts.

Maria's mother had been poor as a girl, compelled to scrape out a living by giving piano lessons. Now that she was a Frau Professor, she wanted to be the best in Göttingen— the best hostess, the best housekeeper, and the best mother. According to family legend, relatives sent her their troublesome children to be taught proper behavior. She ran a "formal" house. She required punctuality and good manners, and hovered over Maria like a hen with an only chick.

But Maria was more her father's daughter than her mother's. He was more interesting to her, she said—"He was after all a scientist." She remembered him as a huge, gentle bear of a man, warmhearted, emotionally open. He had started a free well-baby clinic, and a day nursery for the children of working mothers. These children followed him on the street, calling out to him, clustering at his side.

When Maria was little her father was her favorite companion. They went on science walks together, into the quarries to collect fossils, or to the countryside to learn all the trees and plants by name. In this he was not a typical German Herr Professor. Theirs was an authoritarian society, stiff, class-conscious—a society in which fathers tended to be distant figures who took no part in the lives of little children.

Dr. Goeppert's philosophy of child-rearing was equally atypical. According to Maria, he believed, "The mother is the natural enemy of the child." By this he meant that mothers discouraged daring and risk-taking, that their fears infected the child with fear. He wanted to see boldness, a hunger for adventure. And Maria was not to waste her life. "I mean, he saw so many women who had just played with their children and had no interests whatsoever, and this he didn't like."

Dr. Goeppert's family had produced six generations of university professors; because Maria was the only child, she, too, would have to become a university professor. Although it was never stated in so many words, she'd been aware of this duty as far back as she could recall.

She was eight when World War I put an end to the operas and concerts and dinner parties. Food grew scarce; her father had to feed not only his family, but the children he cared for, and by the time the war was over they were all living on turnip soup, flavored with a pig's ear when Frau Goeppert could find one.

Until the 1920s the university at Göttingen was known chiefly for mathematics, but in the years that followed the war the center shifted. Scientists turned to the exploration of a newly-discovered and invisible world, the world of the very small.

With the birth of atomic physics—the vision of the atom as a planetary system, whose electrons orbited the nucleus—physicists at all European universities drew together in a joint enterprise, one that united them across national boundaries. They were searching for a coherent system that would explain the workings of the atom as clearly and predictably as Isaac Newton had explained the motions of the heavenly bodies.

An atomic physicist named Max Born joined the Göttingen faculty. The Borns and the Goepperts grew to be friends, and Maria became almost a member of the Born household. Max Born remembered her during her years at the university as "pretty, elegant, a high-spirited young lady traveling in the best Göttingen society."

Women accounted for only a tenth of the students at most German universities—in America one-third of the undergraduates were women—but Maria had no trouble being accepted at Göttingen. She was bright and conscientious, and even if she'd had trouble she would not have hesitated to "pull strings." There were advantages to belonging to the best Göttingen society. She thought for a time of going into medicine, but her father talked her out of it "because he always suffered with every child that he lost." In any case she was not like her father, as she realized later. She idolized him but she had more of her mother's temperament—nervous, at times quite shy, and always a perfectionist who demanded too much of herself. She would study mathematics, she decided. She had a natural talent for it, and enjoyed solving problems.

One day Max Born invited Maria to join his physics seminar, a group of students who walked in the hills and ate a rustic supper at one of the village inns, talking physics all the time. The informal atmosphere, as well as the intensity of the students' interest in their subject, was exciting to her. She began to think physics might be more rewarding than mathematics.

There were other reasons for changing fields. During this same period the great developments in quantum mechanics—the laws that govern the atom—were under way, with Göttingen one of the principal centers of research. In fact Göttingen in the mid-1920s might have been described as a "cauldron of quantum mechanics."

It was the greatest intellectual adventure of the 20th century, yet beyond the very small scientific community in Europe, quantum mechanics caused little interest. In America it was only a distant rumor. Even theoretical physics had hardly been heard of in America.

The year 1924, when Maria Goeppert switched to physics, was the year her father died, a blow for which neither she nor her mother was prepared. Now it became her sacred obligation to complete work on her Ph.D. She decided to do it in atomic physics under Max Born, and after that she would find her way as a university professor. There was in fact one woman professor at Göttingen, an illustrious mathematician, who worked solely for the love of it; she received no salary.

The "cauldron of quantum mechanics" that was Göttingen attracted a steady stream of visitors, many with distinguished reputations. Niels Bohr was one, a tall, athletic, soft-spoken Dane, of whom Albert Einstein once said, "He is like an extremely sensitive child who moves around the world in a sort of trance." Bohr's pioneering work on the structure of the atom—for which he had won the Nobel Prize in 1922—placed him in the forefront of atomic physics, and his character was such that he came to be thought of as the conscience of physics.

Younger men came, too, including several Americans in search of the mystery that was quantum mechanics. Joseph E. Mayer arrived in Göttingen in the winter of 1928–29, the coldest winter Europe had seen since Napoleon's time. He was on a Rockefeller grant, his pockets stuffed with Rockefeller money, and the first thing he did was buy a car. "I was a Californian," he said. "What does a Californian do without a car?"

His father had been a bridge engineer, his mother a schoolteacher. Joe was their only child, a thin, gangly six-footer, quick-witted, argumentative, and a tinkerer since boyhood. His training was in experimental chemistry.

Joe went to the Goepperts' house almost as soon as he landed. Like half the inhabitants of Göttingen, the widowed Frau Goeppert took in boarders, and a friend at home had told Joe Mayer it was the only place to live, the most comfortable and attractive—besides, it had the prettiest girl in Göttingen. All the men were in love with her, according to the friend. Most of them had never exchanged two words with Maria, but they loved her from afar.

Joe took a room in the Goepperts' house, and it was just as the friend predicted. He fell in love with Maria and set out to win her, in spite of the heavy competition—perhaps partly because of the competition. She was a challenge, a prize. Slender, blonde, dreamy-eyed, delicately built, she was also "a terrible flirt," according to Joe, ". . . and brighter than any girl I had ever met."

As for Maria, she held back at first. She found Joe likable—everyone found him likable—as well as attractive, considerate, and humorous. But to marry him she would have to leave Göttingen, which meant deserting both her mother and her native land. And America was an unknown world to her. On the other hand, her chances of becoming a university professor in Germany were slim, and might be better in this mysterious America.

So she fell in love by fits and starts, with many hesitations, and could not have chosen more wisely if she'd done it with cool calculation. Joe was delighted at the prospect of a scientist-wife. He meant to help her get wherever she wanted to go, unaware at the beginning that she had it in her power to help him, too.

They married in 1930, and she set to work finishing up her thesis. A "masterpiece of clarity and concreteness," in the opinion of one famous physicist, it took its time in the writing. Joe nudged her; Frau Goeppert did the same. When it was almost ready Maria faced up to the one and only examination a doctoral student in Germany had to take. Her friend Max Delbrück had flunked the examination; he went into biology later and won a Nobel Prize in 1969, but if Delbrück could flunk so could she.

However, the exam was passed, the thesis accepted, and the final break with home could no longer be avoided. One of Maria's aunts encouraged her, explaining that there was bound to be a war. "I have two sons," Aunt Vera said. "They will stay here, and there will be a war and they will die in that war."

But Maria saw no reason to believe in a war. Totally apolitical, unaware of the implications of the bands of Nazi thugs who roamed the streets in their uniforms, she knew only that, whatever her fears of leaving home, she had pledged her word to marry and live in America. She'd be back every summer, she promised her mother, who seemed so brave. She would write several times a week. "Don't miss me too much," Maria said, already aware that she would miss her mother terribly, just as she would miss the forests, the splendid old town, the food, the language, the places that held memories of her father.

———————

Joe had a new appointment in the chemistry department of Johns Hopkins University, in Baltimore, Maryland. Maria, with her Ph.D. from Göttingen, had a little room in the science building, a salary of a few hundred dollars a year for helping a member of the physics department with his German correspondence, and no appointment. Hopkins was not interested in quantum mechanics. Besides, there was the Depression, and the so-called nepotism rule against the hiring of a married couple at the same university. Still Maria had not been prepared for such treatment—"because I was young, I was cocksure of myself; I thought I was good."

Soon after their arrival she set herself the task of teaching quantum mechanics to Joe, or rather the particular approach to quantum mechanics she'd learned from Max Born. According to her letters home, they quarreled constantly during those sessions, which often ended with Maria in tears. She had no stomach for quarrels; even a raised voice caused her distress.

In later years Joe forgot they'd ever quarreled. He remembered only that "I learned all the quantum mechanics I know from her." Around the same period he began teaching his wife physical chemistry, a new and expanding field, and Maria learned from him "chemistry in the sense of the facts. Most theoretical physicists take great pride in not knowing one chemical compound from another."

Later, with one of the graduate students at Hopkins, she did pioneering work on the structure of organic compounds, and in that work applied her special mathematical background, using the methods of group theory and matrix mechanics. A number of papers resulted.

Meanwhile, she was trying to live among Americans. They had rented a tiny row house that could have been fitted into Frau Goeppert's dining room. They searched for a car to replace Joe's "dear little Opel," left behind in Germany. Maria wrote home constantly, devouring her mother's letters, cabling her mother when there was too long a wait between letters. When people asked how she liked America, the best she could truthfully say was, "Not so bad."

However, their summers were free, and they were able to return to Göttingen for three successive years. Maria worked with Max Born, producing an important paper on double-beta decay. Another result was the gradual loss of her illusions about Germany, where everything was old-fashioned, inconvenient, and where she saw her Aunt Vera had been right. Germany was indeed headed for war.

On her return to the United States in 1932 she applied for American citizenship. It was something she had put off doing, but now she was pregnant, and Maria wanted her first child to be born of two American parents. Their daughter Marianne arrived in the spring of 1933, just as the Nazi Party—newly installed in power—declared its first racial laws. Some 200 Jewish teachers and professors were removed from their posts and set adrift in an inhospitable world. Max Born fled to England, others appealed to American friends in the hope of finding sanctuary there.

Soon refugees were making their way to the United States. The Mayers opened their home to a seemingly constant flow of visitors, who were housed and fed for days at a time, in such numbers that Maria later received a thank-you note from a man she could not remember ever having met. One more memorable guest was a young woman physician, who lived with them for several years and helped care for Marianne.

At first Maria had been happy to stay at home with the baby. "It was such an experience to have a child," she said, "such a tremendous experience!" Then, at the end of a year, she returned to work, to physical chemistry and her attic office—and being ignored. Joe wanted to fight for her; he would have delighted in a fight, but she refused to permit it. In time an arrangement was reached that allowed her to give some graduate lectures on a volunteer basis.

A former student remembers that "her facility with the methods of theoretical physics was overwhelming to most of the graduate students, in whom she inspired a considerable amount of awe. At the same time, the students took a rather romantic view of this young scientific couple, known as 'Joe and Maria.' "

The same student describes her as "gracious . . . sympathetic. She was not aggressive—she could speak out, even sharply, but always in a quiet way." However, there was also a certain reserve, an aloofness, and to most people Maria

Mayer was not someone to seek out and confide their troubles to.

There was one man who saw her differently. His name was Edward Teller, in later years known as "the father of the hydrogen bomb," later still as the father of Star Wars. At the time Teller was a young Hungarian refugee, dark-haired, broad-shouldered, with beetling, overhanging brows and a passion for achievement in physics. He had a position at George Washington University, in Washington, D.C., and paid regular visits to Hopkins. With Maria, Teller discussed developments in theoretical physics, especially nuclear physics—the newest, most exciting field, he said.

Maria found in him the ideal mentor, because he had one of the most fertile minds in physics. He loved to talk, he loved teaching; he was patient, humorous, and almost endlessly creative.

But if Maria thought of Teller as a good friend and brilliant teacher, he saw her in a warmer light. In a long series of letters written on trains, in planes, and hotel rooms over the course of many years, Teller opened himself up to her as to a beloved older sister—spilling out his faults and begging absolution for them. He was always late, he got into fights, he yelled at people, he said. He was incurably lazy and inefficient, he said. He envied so-and-so and was ashamed of being envious. He recounted his dreams, his nightmares, his unending self-doubts, his hope that people would say of him after his death, "As a physicist he was moderately lousy, but as a father he was hot stuff." And always he longed to see her—please don't be mad at me, he told her. Please write. "Whatever help and whatever advice I can get from you—I need it."

For Teller, Maria summoned up an infinite supply of sympathy. Impatient with him at times, she nevertheless became what he needed her to be, the kind friend who could always be counted on to listen, to accept and respect him, no matter how many faults he confessed.

Throughout her years at Hopkins, Maria was listed in the university's catalog only as "G"—no name, just that single initial of her maiden name. Her rank was volunteer associate. She worked, was productive, learned from her husband, from Teller, and from some of her colleagues; she wrote two papers on nuclear physics with one of her students, her only forays into this field at the time. But she was not building a career, neither was she wholeheartedly devoted to her profession. And when she became pregnant again, she decided against further teaching. She felt too big, too clumsy. She would write a textbook with Joe instead.

The subject was to be statistical mechanics, a branch of physics concerning the laws that govern assemblies of molecules. They thought of it as a short-term project, but the book took two years to complete—one would write a chapter, the other would write it over, the first would rewrite yet again.

They were still working on it, and Maria was still pregnant, when without warning Joe was fired—or if not fired, encouraged to leave. There had been a temporary breakdown in the physical sciences department; other top men were fired, too. Maria blamed herself, the fact that she always had to be accommodated, made room for. She found the whole affair heartbreaking. But Joe was in no way discouraged. Columbia University offered him a post at twice the Hopkins salary.

Their son Peter was born in 1938, and the following year they left for Columbia. Joe was to be an associate professor in chemistry, while Maria's situation was even worse than it had been in Baltimore. When *Statistical Mechanics* was ready for publication, they needed a title to print under Maria Mayer's name on the front page. A friend brought this up at a departmental meeting. Couldn't some sort of honorary appointment be made, if only for the sake of the book? Apparently it could not, so the friend assigned Maria to give some chemistry lectures, and under her name on the front page, "Lecturer in Chemistry, Columbia University" was printed.

The book became a classic, one that most people believed had been written entirely by Joe.

In 1939, only months before the Mayers left for Columbia, two Europeans arrived in Washington, D.C., to address a conference on theoretical physics. One was Niels Bohr. The other was a short, lively, brilliant young Italian, Enrico Fermi, who had just been awarded the Nobel Prize for research on radioactivity (the process by which atoms give off atomic particles and rays of high energy). Bohr and Fermi brought to America news that was at once thrilling and frightening.

Two German investigators, they said, had discovered what appeared to be nuclear fission. By bombarding uranium atoms with the nuclear particle called a neutron, the nucleus of uranium could be made to split, releasing great energy; this was nuclear fission. Now suppose that the fission process released secondary neutrons and that these could be used to split other uranium nuclei, which would in turn free other neutrons. In that case, tremendous quantities of energy would be generated. A weapon of terrible power could be the result.

Bohr was deeply troubled both about the threat of war in Europe and the implications of nuclear fission.

Maria Mayer and fellow physicists Atkinson and Enrico Fermi.

Enrico Fermi, his wife, Laura, and their two children, then found a house in Leonia, New Jersey, within easy commuting distance of Columbia, where Enrico had an appointment. The Mayers also found a house in Leonia, and the two women became friends. Laura Fermi, who had never seen a dry-cleaning store, sponged and steamed her husband's suits; she had never been to a supermarket, and was terrified of them; she had never done her own gardening. Now Maria took on the task of explaining these mysterious aspects of American life.

Meanwhile Enrico Fermi and others began a long, painful attempt to persuade the U.S. government to begin research into what came to be known as "the uranium problem." By 1941 Fermi had a very small grant for experiments to see whether or not a self-sustaining chain reaction was practical. Maria worked with him, informally, but under a formal oath of secrecy. In December of that year, when the Japanese attack on Pearl Harbor forced the U.S. into World War II, a full-fledged drive to create a fission bomb was set in motion.

Fermi left the following spring for the University of Chicago, where he hoped to build the world's first nuclear reactor. Reactors can be designed to give birth to plutonium, the explosive component of fission bombs. It was the opening act in the drama of the development of the atomic bomb.

———————————

On the day after Pearl Harbor, Maria had accepted a part-time teaching job at Sarah Lawrence College. Almost immediately, Joe also had a new job, investigating conventional weapons at the Aberdeen Proving Grounds in Maryland. He spent five days a week there, a sixth at Columbia, and Sundays at home. Maria was "actively miserable" throughout his absences.

Later that spring she had a second job offer. The chemist Harold Urey (Nobel Prize for chemistry, 1934) was assembling a secret research group at Columbia to separate uranium-235 from the much more abundant uranium-238. U-235 was readily fissionable; U-238 was not. The group was given a code name, Substitute Alloy Materials, and known as SAM. Although SAM was to be housed in Columbia, its actual work would be government work; therefore, Urey was free not only to hire Maria, but to pay her.

Maria found the second job offer overwhelming. She had even been reluctant to work at Sarah Lawrence, since it meant driving to Bronxville, New York, and she worried about being away from her children. Now she was asked to work full time while Joe was far away in Maryland. She'd be depriving the children of both parents. Peter, especially, was a source of concern, a delicate child who always seemed to be coming down with something.

Yet it was impossible to resist a chance to do research, and she finally told Urey she would work part time, and never on Saturdays, although everyone else worked Saturdays, and if the children got sick, she'd insist on staying home. She took temporary leave from Sarah Lawrence, and found a well-educated English girl, stranded in the States by the war, to work as nanny for the children.

As it happened, the children never liked this well-educated English girl. They were used to kindly, affectionate, undereducated German maids, and to their mother, who was extremely permissive. But they never said a word about it to Maria. She was helping win the war, a war being fought not against Germany or the German people, but against Hitler. This had been carefully explained to them. The German people were a wonderful people. Only Hitler was the enemy.

Maria's careful explanations could not, of course, reveal all that was in her heart. Her mother had died a few years earlier, but a large family of aunts, uncles, and cousins remained in Germany. Her fears for them multiplied with D-Day and the Allied invasion of Europe. She kept track of the invading armies by marking their progress on a large wall map. Every pin she put in place stabbed a familiar town or river. Even more troubling than the armies was the bomb that Fermi, Teller, and others were working on—that she herself had been hired to work on. It threatened people she loved, in a country she could not help loving, and she could only pray the war would be over before this bomb was ready.

———————

Maria's job with SAM turned out to be full time after all.

"There were always things that came up; you were supposed to write a report with someone else, who gave it to you at the last minute—and it was lousy. You had to write it over then, write a decent report." Although the work she'd been assigned to was far from the main line of research, the entire SAM project grew, so that where she had had two or three scientists working under her at the start, she ended up with over fifty. And she thoroughly enjoyed both the research and the increased responsibility. "It was the beginning of myself standing on my own two feet as a scientist," she said later, "not leaning against Joe."

The real work of designing the bomb took place at a secret site in Los Alamos, New Mexico, surrounded by guarded, barbed-wire fencing. The laboratory at its center was surrounded by yet another guarded, barbed-wire fence. Some thirty-five miles from Santa Fe in wild, high desert, the place was effectively concealed from the world, which knew nothing about its existence.

Maria made occasional trips there, and was kept informed about every development, always under her oath of secrecy, so that when she saw Joe on Sundays it was necessary to keep everything to herself. Her health began to suffer from the strain. There was a gall-bladder operation, followed by pneumonia; then a thyroid operation. She and Joe had always smoked a good deal, but now she was using a special brand of low-nicotine cigarettes by the name of Carl Henry; convinced these were harmless, she smoked more heavily than ever.

In the spring of 1945 the European war came to an end. At the same time the bomb project was nearing completion, and the whole intricate, costly effort to produce it stood poised on the brink of success, crying out to be tested.

If there was no longer a German enemy on which to use

the bomb, there was the enemy in Japan. When Maria visited Los Alamos later that spring, this was what all the scientists talked about, the forthcoming secret tests of the weapon they had been working on so long and so passionately.

By now Maria had come to hate the whole idea of it, hating the thought of so much destructive power let loose on civilians of whatever nation. In Scotland, Max Born had refused to play any role in the British atomic bomb project. He was the hero of her youth, and it is not surprising that she should have come to conclusions similar to his. There were other American scientists with the same conviction, who asked the Secretary of War to refrain from atomic bombardment of Japan, and to substitute a demonstration of the new weapon on some uninhabited island.

But the machinery was already set in motion. The government, the military, as well as most scientists, had already shifted mental gears so that it now seemed clear the bomb must be used in order to save lives by avoiding a land invasion of Japan.

In mid-July the world's first atomic device was tested in Alamogordo, a remote section of New Mexico, under conditions of utmost secrecy—Maria knew about it, but of course could say nothing to Joe. Then they went to Nantucket and walked on the beach and hunted for clams. She told herself the bomb might not work, knowing all along that this was a vain hope.

The first combat atomic bomb was christened Little Boy. Loaded onto the battle cruiser USS Indianapolis in San Francisco Bay, and borne from there to the Pacific island of Tinian, Little Boy met the B-29 aircraft that was to fly it to

Japan. Paul Tibbetts, who piloted the mission, had named the plane Enola Gay after his mother, Enola Gay Tibbetts.

On the outgoing flight the crew was edgy, fully conscious that they were making history. Drinking coffee and eating ham sandwiches, aware of the smell of hot electronics in the air, they approached Hiroshima. The bomb-bay doors opened and Little Boy floated down over the city. The Enola Gay, now four tons lighter, jumped, then made its turn. As Tibbetts described it, "A bright light filled the plane. The first shock wave hit us. We were eleven-and-a-half miles slant range from the atomic explosion but the whole airplane cracked and crinkled from the blast. . . . [One of the crew] said he could taste atomic fission. He said it tasted like lead."

In Hiroshima, as scientists learned later, the temperature at the site of explosion reached 5400 degrees Fahrenheit. Many people were immediately incinerated; many were to die afterwards of radiation poisoning. Recent estimates place the number of deaths, up to the end of 1945, at 140,000.

In England Otto Hahn, one of the two German scientists who first demonstrated the possibility of nuclear fission, was "shocked and depressed without measure" when he first heard of the bombing. Other scientists were elated. Still others, like Maria, felt a vague but haunting sense of guilt. For the rest of her life she was grateful that she had not worked directly on the bomb, and yet the guilt still clung to her.

———————

Peace, quite suddenly, was upon them. Maria's job with Urey no longer existed, and she returned to part-time teaching at Sarah Lawrence. There would be time now for the children, a chance to make up for what she thought of as years of neglect.

Then Joe was offered a full professorship at the University of Chicago. Fermi, Teller, and Urey were going, too. Maria said yes, of course he must accept. And no sooner had he replied to Chicago than Maria was also invited. She was to be a voluntary associate professor, without salary, but she was wanted, expected. There would be an office of her own; she was to participate fully in the life of the university. Touched, immensely grateful, Maria never forgot that this was "the first place where I was not considered a nuisance, but greeted with open arms."

They left triumphantly for Chicago and started house-hunting. She had never really liked Leonia, she said. "I don't like suburbs. The women all talked about their babies, and the men talked science." This time they would live in the city.

On Chicago's South Side, the no-longer-fashionable side, they found a big old house with five bathrooms, six fireplaces, a third floor that had once been a ballroom, and space outdoors for several gardens. Maria fell in love with the place. They immediately arranged to buy it, and never for a moment regretted the decision. In time Joe built a greenhouse upstairs, on a balcony attached to the ballroom. Maria grew orchids there. It was one of the many pleasures that awaited them in Chicago.

The best was an offer that came within months of their arrival. Maria was invited to be a senior physicist at the Argonne National Laboratory, newly established and attached to the university. She would work part time in the theoretical physics division, and she would be paid for her work. Sixteen years had passed since Maria earned her Ph.D., and only now did she have a peacetime job, an office, a salary, as well as colleagues who recognized her as their equal.

A former student of Joe's remembers him as "the only scientist I've known who had such a broad view of science." He had already made important contributions to the theories of liquids and solutions; partly because of Maria's influence, he had also worked on the quantum mechanics of atoms and molecules. Lively, always open to new ideas, he asked penetrating questions and encouraged younger scientists to speak up.

For these reasons Joe was chosen to take charge of the weekly science seminar at the university's Institute for Nuclear Studies. He decided to run it like a Quaker meeting: "anybody who has anything to say, he'll talk about it," and talk as long as he liked, unless effectively interrupted—for five minutes or for twenty.

Under Joe's direction the science seminars brought together some of the greatest scientists of their generation; one observer recalled that being with them "was like sitting in on a conversation of the angels."

Maria attended the seminars but said nothing at first. She kept her own counsel and listened intently. She was there to learn. The chief interest of the institute was nuclear physics, a field in which she had little experience. In fact, her entire career thus far had been a series of part-time ventures. So she set herself the task of learning nuclear physics by a kind of absorption process at the weekly seminars.

The first few times she understood nothing at all. After that, "I went to those seminars and asked two questions after each one. And no more than two. And I'd better assimilate the answer to those two questions."

The questions were usually addressed to Teller, sometimes to Fermi. Many of the scientists at Chicago had been working on nuclear problems since before the war, as Teller had, and a whole language had grown up during the war years, one that was commonplace to nuclear physicists but a mystery to Maria. Joe remembered her telling him after one seminar that something had been said about a thimble. Everyone else knew what it was, but Maria had to devote one of her two questions to this thimble. "The thimble is a hole in the reactor," Joe said "but what did that mean to Maria?"

Maria had been at Chicago for about a year when Teller came to her with an idea that fascinated him, a theory about the origin of the elements. He needed someone to work with—a sociable person, Teller never enjoyed working alone—and chose Maria not only for the pleasure of her company, but for her ability to do the complex mathematics involved. As always Maria welcomed the chance to work with Teller.

His theory was in line with beliefs current at the time, that most elements had been formed when the universe was very young, perhaps as part of a creation process—a belief that has since been discarded.

Soon both Teller and Maria began to be struck by the fact that a few elements—tin and lead, for example—were much more abundant than their theory explained. They discussed this at length, wandering in and out of each other's offices. For an element to be extremely abundant meant it had a very stable nucleus; the unstable ones lose or gain electrons and thus form new chemical combinations—that is, they change into other elements. And why were those particular nuclei, the lead and the tin and the others, so remarkably stable?

Teller went out of town, leaving Maria to think about the abundant nuclei on her own. She noticed that "in these nuclei either the number of protons or the number of neutrons were very special." Protons and neutrons are the particles that make up the nucleus.

All the abundant nuclei had either 82 or 50 neutrons, or else 82 or 50 protons. More special numbers were to turn up later.

When Teller returned he was no longer interested in the origin of the elements, and Maria took her questions mainly to Fermi. People began referring to her "magic numbers," a phrase that was originally used by the physicist Eugene Wigner, who considered them charming nonsense, but Maria used the same phrase herself. She believed the numbers were indeed magical. In any case Fermi took them seriously, and so did Joe.

To the original two she had added others, so that there was now a total of seven: 2, 8, 20, 28, 50, 82, and 126. Any element with a magic number's worth of protons or neutrons was extremely stable. And as the numbers had increased, so had the mystery deepened.

Month after month Maria spent much of her working day with the numbers, either discussing them with Fermi or collecting data from nuclear experimentalists, men who worked at the cyclotron—an "atom-smasher"—or the nuclear reactor, which is much like the core of a nuclear power plant. And over and over again, their accounts proved to be studded with the very same numbers.

Maria would come home evenings in a state of high excitement. Flinging herself into an armchair, she talked non-stop about her numbers, and Joe would listen, and nod, and tell her to keep on accumulating numbers—even though there was no explanation, even though they were "magic," uncomfortable for theorists, who wanted explanations, not facts. The numbers were magic, but they were also real.

"I never got rid of thinking, what are they?" she recalled. "They lived with me for a year."

Working full-time now, captivated by her numbers, she was never able to give the children the kind of attention she had hoped to give them. Her social life changed as well; the Mayers had always been hospitable, and Maria still entertained on a liberal scale, but less often now, with a few big parties taking the place of many small ones. Laura Fermi remembered the Maria of those days as being different from the companionable woman she had known in Leonia. "My impression is that faculty wives like me did no longer have easy access to Maria Mayer, because she was always talking to the men and had a too technical conversation."

As for the men—Enrico Fermi, Teller, Urey and others—they thoroughly enjoyed Maria's technical conversation; she listened more than she talked, as one of them pointed out later, but she listened so attractively, and was so lovely to look at.

At work, however, several of her colleagues remained openly skeptical of her numbers, especially as Maria had begun to consider a shell model of the nucleus.

She described it as somewhat like an onion, in layers, with the protons and neutrons revolving around each other and forming the shells of the onion. In other words, the nucleus resembles the planetary atom.

And this resemblance explains why the persistence of the "magic numbers" led Maria to think of a shell model for the nucleus—for there are certain magically stable numbers in ordinary atomic physics. Helium, neon, argon, krypton and xenon—all gases—are called the "five noble gases" because their orbiting electrons are so tightly bound to the nucleus that they do not readily change into other elements. Each of the five noble gases may be said to have magic numbers of electrons.

Maria's shell model was a good, sound, interesting idea, although not an entirely original one, since others had considered a shell model for the nucleus and rejected it, in the 1930s. But she had now accumulated many more magic numbers, and in April 1948 she published a paper on the subject in *Physical Review*. There were no new theories in it, no fresh illuminations, but there were vast amounts of new and recent information from experimentalists working with cyclotrons and reactors.

One day Maria and Fermi were in Maria's office, talking shell model as usual. All that had come of their many hours of talk was that one paper, but this time Fermi had some new ideas to offer.

Before he could put them into words, someone knocked on the door. A head appeared in the doorway, to say that Professor Fermi was wanted on the phone in his office. Fermi rose to go, and as he started for the doorway he said to Maria, "What about spin-orbit coupling?"

Maria said, "Yes, Enrico, that's the solution." She knew it instantly—there was an almost bodily feeling, an awesome sensation she was never quite able to describe, one that was so forceful it wiped everything else out of her mind.

"How can you know?" Fermi asked as he went through the door. But she had already taken up pencil and paper and started the calculations to prove what her body told her had to be right.

As Joe recalled it, Fermi came back less than ten minutes later "and Maria started to 'snow' him with the detailed explanation. Maria, when excited, had a rapid-fire oral delivery, whereas Enrico always wanted a slow, detailed, and methodical explanation. Enrico smiled and left: 'Tomorrow, when you are less excited, you can explain it to me.' "

Spin-orbit coupling can be pictured in the following way, as Maria once told Marianne: Think of a roomful of waltzers. Suppose they go round the room in circles, each circle enclosed within another.

Then imagine that in each shell, or circle, you can fit twice as many dancers by having one pair go clockwise, the other counterclockwise. Then add one more variation: all the dancers are spinning—twirling—round and round like tops as they circle the room, each pair both twirling and circling. But only some of those that go counterclockwise are twirling counterclockwise; the others are twirling clockwise while circling counterclockwise. The same is true of those that are dancing around clockwise: some twirl clockwise, others twirl counterclockwise.

So do the nuclear particles. And there is an important difference in the energy a particle needs to twirl one way, as compared to twirling the other way. "Anyone who has ever danced the fast waltz knows that it's easier to spin one way around than the other," as Maria puts it. Working with this new vision, she saw that this was both the explanation of the magic numbers, and proof of the shell theory of the nucleus. With spin-orbit coupling the number of possible paths along which the nuclear particles could travel increased. And wherever a shell was most tightly bound in place, there were the magic numbers.

Think of them—the numbers—as representing the number of dancers who form a completed circle, very stable, with just enough room for themselves. This circle resists being broken into by any extra dancer passing by. In effect, the number of dancers represents the number of nuclear particles in a shell.

When she told Joe about it he said, "You must publish immediately!" She explained this was not such an easy matter. Two of the physicists who had done shell model work before had sent her a pre-print of a paper they were ready to publish, a paper also offering a shell model, although different from her own. Maybe their new paper was inspired by her "magic number" paper. Maybe not. But it didn't seem right to her to publish now, having seen their pre-print and knowing they'd done their work first.

Joe told her this was nonsense, but she went ahead and put together a short report, so brief it took the form of a Letter to the Editor rather than a paper, and sent it to *Physical Review* with the request that it be published in the same issue as the competing shell model paper.

During the next few months Joe repeatedly urged her to write it up properly, at length, and with all the supporting data she had spent months piling up and meticulously analyzing. He couldn't understand her modesty. Courtesy to colleagues was one thing, but this holding back, this hiding of a brilliant new idea—no, he could not understand it. Neither could Teller, who was no longer a partner in the work, but remained as always interested in whatever interested Maria.

However, Maria was different from Joe and Teller. To begin with, she was modest and almost self-effacing, a person who lacked aggressiveness, disliked arguments and hot competition, and saw no value in getting ahead by beating out someone else, even though this was the accepted style among scientists, certainly accepted by Joe and Teller. Furthermore, as a working scientist she was used to being tolerated, just barely tolerated. Therefore, neither her personality nor her experience encouraged her to speak up.

Joe grew impatient and began haranguing her. Marianne remembers a day when her parents were both in the little downstairs study, Joe pacing up and down from the study to the living room, to the entry, then back. Finally he said, "For God's sake, Maria, write it up!" And his voice was so sharp, so peremptory, that Marianne went to look through the open doorway, aware that he never spoke to her mother in quite that way.

She saw him putting a pencil in her mother's hand, holding the pencil to paper, and standing over Maria until she started to write. The article was not finished in that one session but it was certainly begun. By December of 1949 it had taken the form of two full-length papers describing the shell model and the experimental data that backed it up.

One month before the articles were to be published, *Physical Review* carried another shell model paper, with an almost identical interpretation of the magic numbers. Its authors were Hans Jensen, of Heidelberg, Germany, and two colleagues.

Maria's initial reaction was profound disappointment at not being the first and only discoverer, but on second thought she realized that if this Jensen came to the same conclusion independently, that must mean she was right. Fermi assured her she was right; he had been teaching her shell model to his students from the moment it was born.

Moreover, the physics community recognized that Jensen's work and Maria's had been done simultaneously. Although there were many who still doubted its value, some of them distinguished scientists, she was consoled by the knowledge that she had not lost first place after all. She was simply sharing it. Of course if Joe hadn't bullied her into writing the two long papers, Jensen would have had first place to himself, and she would have had—what? A valuable experience.

She began corresponding with Jensen. In a series of letters written with formal correctness, Maria referred to "our theory," while he gallantly spoke of "your theory." He added that physicists in Europe, including Niels Bohr, had no doubt about its value.

Then, in 1950, Joe and Maria had a chance to visit Germany under U.S. State Department sponsorship. Maria knew it would be painful to go—to confront the wartime losses, to meet those fellow scientists who had stayed, while wondering which of them cooperated with the Hitler regime—but she also longed to go. Teller was afraid for her. "I do not know what will happen and I do not think we should be too cautious," he wrote, "but, please, do not go to Berlin."

They did go to Berlin, and a year later Maria returned to Germany on her own. From these visits she learned that Göttingen was essentially unharmed; it had been declared a hospital city and was therefore protected from fire bombing. Some other cities had suffered horribly—there was terrible devastation in Frankfurt, for example. But Maria's extended family was mostly intact. And she met Hans Jensen, who proved to be utterly unlike his stiff, formal letters.

Maria took to him immediately, finding him mischievous, humorous, a great tease. His parents had been working-class people, his father a gardener. Jensen went to university only through a fluke, and never really believed in his good fortune at becoming an educated man. Much loved by his students, he dressed like a student, in a ragbag collec-

The year was 1953. World War II had been over for eight years when Maria and her husband Joe Mayer visited Japan. Maria had helped develop the atomic bomb that was dropped on Japan in 1945.

tion of clothing, and there seemed to be little he took seriously—not even work. He had a couch in his office and napped on it whenever he liked.

Maria and Jensen continued their correspondence after her return from Europe, and now his letters were affectionate, even flirtatious, with bits of poetry and passages from novels sandwiched in between physics. One letter finishes,

"Yours sincerely, the scamp, the spoiled boy . . ." while another ends, "With love, your twin brother."

They planned to write a book together about their shell model. Since this would be difficult to do by mail, Maria set about finding ways for Jensen to visit the United States, and when he did so he stayed with the Mayers for a time. They did a great deal of talking about their book, but Jensen's easygoing habits—his laziness—held up production of an actual book.

Maria wrote her share, then most of Jensen's as well. Joe stood by as sounding board, editor, and cheerleader. There were even times, he recalled, when he had felt himself drawn into the work, ready to succumb to his interest in it and become a partner. Yet he saw unmistakably that Maria—usually so self-effacing—was letting him know: Hands off, this is mine.

During the four years it took to write the book, the Mayer-Jensen shell model came to be accepted throughout the physics community, on both sides of the ocean. The book only confirmed its importance.

Enrico Fermi died of cancer in 1954, only months before his fifty-third birthday. Of his death, Maria said, "He endured it with the greatest grace you can imagine." For her, as for all the Chicago group, it was a huge loss. The heart seemed to go out of things with Fermi's death. Soon people were drifting away to other destinations. When Joe and Maria were offered posts at the University of California's new San Diego campus, they accepted with eagerness.

Maria was now a full professor, with a new house in La Jolla, a new garden to establish, a new department to help build. But soon after her arrival in California she suffered a stroke that left one arm paralyzed. Her health continued to deteriorate. She tired easily but she never stopped smoking—it was too late to stop.

On a November morning in 1963, at 4 A.M., the phone rang. It was a call from Stockholm for Maria Mayer, who was still partly asleep, and murmured into the receiver, "But I don't know anyone in Stockholm." Joe went quickly to the kitchen and put some champagne on ice.

With Hans Jensen, Maria had won half the prize in physics, the other half going to Eugene Wigner, who had once been so skeptical of her magic numbers, for work in quantum mechanics. The Mayers phoned Peter, then Marianne. They had a breakfast of bacon and eggs and champagne, Maria still finding it hard to believe. She was the only woman besides Marie Curie to win the Nobel for physics.

Reporters and camera crews began arriving. Friends phoned. Telegrams and flowers were delivered. For the next forty-eight hours their home was under siege. "La Jolla Mother Wins Nobel Prize," announced a local newspaper, a bit of condescension that amused Maria.

Old friends in Germany were asked to comment about Maria Goeppert-Mayer, and usually remarked that she had been the beauty of Göttingen. When American friends were interviewed they described her marvelous parties, her enviable garden. At a press conference on the lawn of the San Diego campus, the morning after the announcement, Joe and Maria posed side by side for photographers. Joe was asked a few questions. Did he think of the woman beside him as a wife, or as a scientist? He looked around, startled, and answered, "Why a wife, of course."

Afterwards Maria went on with her teaching and her gardening, cherishing the orchids that grew out-of-doors now. In her sixties she had the same very blue eyes, with the same dreamy expression in them, that the early pictures show. Her hair was tinted auburn, her complexion still lovely, but she had grown quite frail. Her right arm was limp and her speech sometimes difficult to follow.

As for Joe, he had hardly changed; he was brisk, energetic, humorous, and, as always, protective of Maria.

To Maria it was always clear that everything would have been different without Joe. It was Joe who wanted her to work, Joe who begged to be allowed to fight for her. When the children were little and she was tempted to stay at home, Joe insisted that with part-time help, the job of running a household, overseeing children, and entertaining on a lavish scale should take no more than a couple of hours a day.

He had helped in other ways as well, by encouraging her early work with the magic numbers, by bullying her into writing the two papers. And when she sat on the flower-filled platform at the Nobel ceremony she watched him in the audience below, where he looked "enchanting." Wearing white tie and tails he had borrowed from their son Peter, he caught her eye and began to weep unashamedly.

During the last years of her life Maria's health continued to decline and she died of a heart attack nine years later at the age of sixty-six.

Rosalyn Yalow

CHAPTER 2

ROSALYN YALOW:

1977 Nobel Prize for Medicine

"A SUGAR CUBE IN LAKE ERIE"

Coming home from the subway with her arms full of textbooks, her head full of a long day's lectures, Ros heard a voice from the kitchen that pushed her back into childhood. It was her mother's voice, telling a story against a background of clattering teacups. They'd be sitting at the kitchen table, her mother and the neighbor women she was telling this story to.

Ros had heard the story so many times that she knew every word, every lifted eyebrow or little smile that went with each word. It began with the day when Alex, her older brother, went to school for the first time and came back crying. Rivers of tears poured out of him. Mother asked why, what happened.

He said the teacher took a ruler and whacked him across the knuckles; she was strict, the strict teachers did things like that when they thought you'd stepped out of line.

Then the day came when Ros had this same teacher— so the story went—and it happened again; the teacher took up a ruler and whacked Ros across the knuckles. Did Ros cry? Did she pour out rivers? Not Ros. She snatched the ruler and whacked the teacher back.

There was a little pause at this point in the narrative—there always was—to give the listeners a chance to gasp. In that world of immigrant parents, school was a sacred place, and teachers were powerful beings who spoke pure English, without a trace of accent, so it was no small matter to defy a teacher. Then Mother's voice went on, smooth as silk, telling how Ros was sent to the principal's office. The principal asked why she had done such a thing.

And Ros told him she'd been waiting for years to do it, ever since the teacher hit Alex.

A silence followed, same as always. Ros tiptoed down the hall to her bedroom, picturing the faces of the women to whom her mother was telling the story now. She herself was not sure that it had really happened, or happened in exactly that way; she had no memory of it, only the memory of her mother's telling it, proudly, with great relish. As if to say: "You see what kind of daughter I have. A good girl, smart—maybe not so smart as her brother, but this is how she's different from him and everyone else. She's tough and stubborn, that one. He comes home crying, she goes and hits the teacher back."

Rosalyn Sussman Yalow was born in 1921, in the South Bronx, the second child of Simon Sussman and his wife, Clara. They were poor, but in America being poor was not necessarily permanent. You worked hard, saved a little, added more to that little and invested it somewhere, until one day you moved out of the walkup apartment, maybe into one of those big houses on the Grand Concourse. Such things were possible in America.

Another part of Rosalyn's family lived across the

street—three aunts, two unmarried, while the oldest, Aunt Rose, had a husband and daughter. They all lived together with Rosalyn's grandmother, who had brought them from Germany when Clara was small. Some years later, at the age of twelve, Clara left school and went to work as a cashier in a department store.

These were vigorous, healthy, capable women, destined to live well into their nineties, and the two families lived as if they were one family.

As for Simon Sussman's people, they came from the Ukraine in Russia to New York's Lower East Side, the heartland of American Jewry, where Simon was born. Having finished eighth grade, he had two more years of schooling than his wife. Like all the mothers of their neighborhood, Clara stayed home, while Simon, like all the fathers, went out every morning in a dark suit, white shirt, and tie to earn a living, which meant doing battle with the world, usually in factories or sweatshops. Simon Sussman worked hard, six days a week, again like all the fathers. He had started his own one-man business in paper and twine—a serious person, matter-of-fact, who read *The New York Times* every day. He had a streak of stubbornness that Ros inherited. She thought she might have inherited his quickness with numbers as well—he did all his own bookkeeping. "These people," his daughter explains, "they weren't educated in the schools. But they were educated. They did it themselves."

In the Sussman home there was money for Saturday afternoon movies, for roller skates, for occasional baseball games on Sunday, when Ros's father took her with him to Yankee Stadium. Other things were free, such as the public library; Alex was sent with his little sister once each week, to return old books and trade them in for new ones. She enjoyed reading, but was by nature sociable, and there was always something going on in the street—neighborhood children played for hours in the streets. Boys had boys' games, girls had games of their own—jacks, hopscotch, dolls, keeping house. Ros preferred girls' games and the company of girls, and never owned a chemistry set, never thought of wanting one. Her family couldn't have afforded it if she had.

Simon Sussman had been investing in the stock market—not much, since he didn't have much, and he invested carefully. And when the stock market fell apart in October of 1929, and rich men threw themselves out of the upper-story windows of Manhattan buildings because they couldn't face being no longer rich, Mr. Sussman lost his savings. But he was able to hold on to the business. By early 1930 bread-lines in Manhattan's Bowery district were drawing 2,000 people a day. The Depression was nationwide, even world-wide. With the breadwinners out of work, whole families found themselves out on the street, along with their few sticks of furniture, for nonpayment of rent. There was no unemployment insurance, no medical insurance, no welfare system.

The Sussmans were lucky; they knew they would climb back. They were still young, willing to work hard, and they were sustained by their dreams—not for themselves but for the children, who were bright, and deserved to go on to college. Ros, for example, had taught herself to read before she started kindergarten. Once in school she showed an unusual aptitude for arithmetic. She skipped grades several times. And when extra money was needed—among other things, for orthodontia, because her teeth would one day require it—she was ready to help. One of her uncles was "in neck-wear," meaning he manufactured women's collars, and her father began bringing home cut sections of fabric for her mother to sew. "At eight I started doing what they called 'homework.' " Dr. Yalow recalls. "I would turn the cut pieces of cloth while my mother would press."

By junior high Ros was essentially grown, dark-haired, with big dark eyes under strongly marked brows, and bossy—a take-charge person. She dressed well, mostly in clothing made by her mother. She cared about her appearance, cared about being in style, and every now and then an opportunity came, like a gift from the almost-unknown world beyond the Bronx, to own a dress that was not homemade.

In that neighborhood where everyone knew everyone else, one of the women went from time to time to S. Klein's in Manhattan, an off-price outlet for women's clothing. This meant a long ride by subway. The subway meant a nickel each way, and nobody spent that much to buy just one dress, Dr. Yalow explains. "She would bring home ten to twenty one-dollar dresses. They were gorgeous, those dresses. Then all the neighbors came in and tried on whatever they liked. No matter what size or color, there was always someone who wanted them. They would pay her back, but nothing extra—she didn't do it to make a profit, but because she enjoyed this sort of thing. . . . There was a very close neighborhood interaction. We were all poor together, and everybody helped one another."

Junior high was a girls-only school—"P.S. 10 Junior High, we had very good girls there," Ros recalled. Then she went on to Walton High, again for girls only. She took geometry, and the head of the math department immediately placed her under his wing, giving her extra math education. She decided she was in love with math and would devote her life to it. But the year after that she took chemistry, and this teacher also took her under his wing, so she decided she'd become a chemist. Logic was what fascinated her, the solving of puzzles to get at the logical structure behind them.

Among her friends there were several others interested in science. They would talk about it, about how they were going to be "big-deal scientists," utterly single-minded and caring only about work. They never mentioned marriage. But Ros Sussman was going to marry and become a scientist, both. It was a settled matter in her mind. Since the age of thirteen she'd been going out with boys, on the lookout for someone "willing to put up with me," by which she meant someone ready to take on a difficult, stubborn, bossy person.

She never thought of herself as brighter than the others; her friends were all bright girls, she says. But she was more assertive. "I'm a tough baby," she told a reporter once. And lucky, for being in the right place at the right time, and for having wonderful teachers who pushed her.

At fifteen she was graduated from Walton and entered Hunter College, an exceptional institution, tuition-free, open to any young woman who lived in New York and had competitive high school grades. The gifted daughters of the immigrant generation went to Hunter, and often the daughters of the middle class as well. It was a school with a long tradition of support for women in the professions.

Although she'd planned to major in chemistry, in her sophomore year Ros took her first college-level physics course, and from then on physics was all she cared about. Reading *Madame Curie,* the biography of a woman whose life was enriched and fulfilled by a fierce devotion to physics, only served to confirm the decision. Everyone was reading the book, everyone was stirred by it, but at Hunter the one person determined to major in physics was Ros Sussman. There were a number of excellent physics teachers, but they did not offer a physics major; there was too little demand for it, so they gave only enough physics to satisfy math and chemistry majors who wanted to minor in physics. This didn't trouble her at all. A Hunter classmate remembers Ros as "very single-minded. She knew—*absolutely knew*—she was going to become a physicist. She told this to anyone who would listen."

Her parents had trouble understanding the new love affair. To begin with, they weren't sure what physics was, or how it was done, and she wanted not only to become a physicist but to do research in physics. Extraordinary things had been happening in the field since the late 1920s, most of them concerned with the atom, its particles, its nucleus, and the mechanics that governed the way it worked.

But the man in the street had never heard of the atom or its nucleus. The man in the street was busy earning a living in hard times. According to Dr. Yalow, her parents' dearest wish was that she would become an elementary school teacher like her older cousin, because "that's what Jewish girls did in those days." They married, had children, and lived in the neighborhood. As for earning a Ph.D. and doing research, "It was an unknown life, as far as my parents were concerned."

Ros joined the Physics Club, was elected vice-president, and had her picture taken for the yearbook seated in the front row, legs very straight, hands primly clasped, a broad smile revealing strong white teeth perfected by orthodontia. Some of the club members went with her to hear Enrico

Fermi—Nobel laureate in physics, 1938—when he spoke at Columbia University on the eve of World War II. Fermi described the discovery by two German investigators of what seemed to be nuclear fission, the possibility of starting a chain reaction by splitting the atom. A new world was being born; she would live to see it, to read about it, perhaps even take an active part in it. Why not? When you set your heart on something and worked toward that something, your eyes fixed on that one goal and never wavering, surely nothing could stop you.

At the beginning of her senior year Hunter College decided she could, after all, major in physics. "Basically they started the physics major just for me," she explains. She had to go to City College at night for an extra course, and even then her background was spotty, "but they were very pleased with me." She says this with a quick defensive smile, as if to deny she was in any way special, and hurries to add that in those days there were many bright women at Hunter. Five later became members of the National Academy of Sciences.

Then the search began for a graduate school willing to admit her as a teaching assistant—a student and teacher, with a stipend to live on, and no tuition fees.

Letters of application went out. One prestigious Midwest university replied that since she was a Jew, and a woman, they would never be able to get her a job. If her physics professor could guarantee that she would not become their responsibility once she finished her education, they were willing to grant the assistantship.

Of course no such guarantee was possible. "My professors were very honest with me; they said it's not really likely you'll do better elsewhere." But Dr. Jerrold Zacharias made an unusual suggestion. His wife, who had a job at Columbia's medical school, could get Ros work as secretary to a biochemist there. She was already an excellent typist, she need only promise to learn stenography, and once she was in, she'd be able to attend graduate-level courses in physics.

Columbia permitted its nonfaculty employees— whether secretaries, lab technicians, or janitors, anyone who worked full-time for the university—to take classes without paying tuition. It was called "the back door." Just as an unsuccessful applicant for medical school nowadays might take a job in a laboratory at that school—hoping to catch the eye of some professor, reapply, and be accepted with the professor's recommendation—so did Ros Sussman hope to squeeze into Columbia through the back door.

So halfway through her senior year she began work as a secretary to the biochemist, who was of German origin. "I was an excellent typist," she said. "I could read German— I'd taken two years of scientific German in college, and before that, remember, I came from a German family; until I was ten my grandmother had spoken German to me." In other words, she took her secretarial job seriously, and was proud of doing well at it.

Then she graduated from Hunter in January 1941, magna cum laude, Phi Beta Kappa, and started evening classes in stenography at the Monroe Business School. Six weeks later a letter from the University of Illinois at Urbana admitted her as a graduate assistant. Her joy at this news can be imagined from the fact that thirty-five years later, in a brief biography written for the Nobel Prize Committee, she called her acceptance "an achievement beyond belief."

America had not yet entered World War II, but the draft of young men into the armed forces had already begun, and this greatly increased her chances at Illinois. Never mind the reason; she was in, the dreamed-of life was underway.

The university was going to pay her $70 a month. "I was a rich woman," she said. She continued her secretarial job until June of 1941, and left in the fall for Urbana.

She had just turned twenty, a quick-thinking, quick-talking, determined young woman, with a warmth that showed itself only to those closest to her. In Illinois she meant to find a husband, a physicist-husband, she told her mother before she went.

At Illinois she was the only woman among 400 faculty and teaching assistants in the College of Engineering, and one of three Jews in the entering physics group. Aaron Yalow was another. They met on the first day of school.

A rabbi's son from upstate New York, he proved to be "very bright, with an unusual sense of humor," she says. "He punned a good deal. He was relaxed. He read . . . everything." Thoughtful, tolerant, easygoing, Aaron Yalow was nevertheless a complex person, a scientist who remained throughout his life an Orthodox Jew, and they looked at one another with lively interest that first day.

Otherwise, it was not an easy time. With the best will in the world Hunter had not prepared her for the level of course work at Illinois. She decided to sit in on two undergraduate courses without credit, while taking three graduate courses, and working as a part-time teaching assistant. In December of that year Pearl Harbor brought the country into the war. The campus filled with students sent by the Army and Navy for training; half the young faculty left for secret scientific work elsewhere, while those who remained found the teaching load heavy, with little time for sleep, and none for recreation or socializing. And the head of the physics department—acting head, actually—made no secret of the fact that he'd been against admitting even one woman.

Rosalyn Yalow and her husband Aaron working on their home computer.

But Aaron and Ros were together—their studies threw them together. She learned he expected to keep a kosher home after he married, while he had a chance to see if he cared to spend his life with a stubborn, take-charge woman, one who would never be content as "just a housewife."

They married in 1943, in June, the marrying month. It was also the month when Aaron took his "general," an exam given orally by five professors. Nobody ever flunks a general—the incompetent students have been weeded out much earlier in the graduate school process—but it is an awesome experience, the lone student facing the five professors. And in Aaron's case one of the professors was the acting department chairman. His resentment of Ros spilled over onto her new husband.

The chairman asked Aaron a question; when Aaron answered, the chairman claimed he was wrong, "and my husband was insecure enough that he proved his answer in twelve different ways ... maybe it was ten, maybe twenty, I don't remember."

When Ros took her exam in September the chairman tried the same tactic. "My answer was, 'Goldhaber and Nye taught it to me this way, so if there's anything wrong you better talk to them about it.' The guy walked right out of my exam and didn't come back."

Professors Maurice Goldhaber and Herbert Nye were there when she said it. They knew, as she did, that the chairman had behaved like a child, but the exam went on as if the incident had never taken place. Looking back on it, Yalow says she'd do it again. "I was right, I knew what I was doing. I wasn't going to be troubled by that guy."

Maurice Goldhaber was married to a physicist, Gertrude Scharff-Goldhaber, who had to work as an unpaid research assistant until the end of the 1940s, so he knew firsthand that the university was unjust to women, destructive of women's talents, and he was openly sympathetic to women students. Both Aaron and Ros had chosen him to supervise their doctorates, not for that reason alone—Goldhaber was a highly talented physicist—but it was a consideration.

When Ros completed her thesis, Aaron was still working on his, so she went on alone to New York to find a job.

With her mother the new Dr. Yalow paid a visit to her paternal grandmother, still living in the fourth-floor walkup apartment in the Bronx. When she saw them this ninety-four-year-old woman dashed down four flights of stairs to the candy store, and returned with three ice-cream sodas in her hands.

The Bronx had hardly changed. It would change drastically in the postwar years, but for now it seemed as if the old neighborhoods, and the tough, vibrant, enduring people who gave them their flavor, were to last forever. After three-and-a-half years in foreign parts, Ros Yalow was back on her own territory. She hoped never to leave it again.

When Aaron joined her they rented a small Manhattan apartment, and found work as assistant engineers at a federal laboratory. But the research group in which they were working left New York in 1946; they had to split up, Aaron going to New York State Maritime College, while Ros returned to Hunter, to teach physics. One of her students later recalled that she was "spectacular" as a teacher.

But she had dreamed of a future in physics research; there were no research facilities at Hunter. Moreover, her summers were free, and free time, especially a summer of it, was not for her. She needed to be hard at work—she loved work, had an actual passion for it, and was always happiest when her capacities were strained to the limit.

In the summer of 1947 she began casting about for "something useful to occupy my time," research of some kind, perhaps even unpaid.

———————————

An isotope is a variant form of an atom. A radioisotope is a radioactive variant. Irène Joliot-Curie, Marie Curie's scientist daughter, and her husband, Frédéric Joliot, won the Nobel in 1935 for making artificial radioactive elements, but it was a difficult and expensive process, until the invention of the nuclear reactor, by Enrico Fermi and others, during the course of their war research. Medical radioisotopes can be made plentifully in a nuclear reactor.

In those postwar years everyone was talking about "Atoms for Peace"—constructive uses for the nuclear fission that destroyed Hiroshima. They meant medical uses, chiefly, and Aaron had been working as a part-time consultant in medical physics for Montefiore Hospital. It occurred to him that this could be the ideal field for his wife, a field that was new, uncrowded, but headed for rapid expansion. He suggested a visit to Dr. Edith Quimby, a medical physicist at Columbia.

It proved to be a fruitful suggestion, more so than either Aaron or Ros could have imagined. "I volunteered to work in [Dr. Quimby's] laboratory to gain research experience. . . . She took me to see 'The Chief,' Dr. G. Failla, dean of American medical physicists. After talking to me for a while, he picked up the phone, dialed, and I heard him say, 'Bernie, if you want to set up a radioisotope service, I have someone here you must hire.' Dr. Bernard Roswit, Chief of the Radiotherapy Service at the Bronx Veterans Administration Hospital and I appeared to have no choice; Dr. Failla had spoken."

When Yalow thinks back on it now it seems remarkable that she was offered such a job. At twenty-six she looked far younger. One of the Columbia professors remembered her as "a cheerful little person, not at all imposing," and she had never taken a biology course, never had postdoctoral training—none of the things that are considered necessary nowadays to become an investigator. But because Failla was impressed, she had a job, a salary, and the chance of a career in research.

On a December day, during the great blizzard of 1947, she joined the Bronx VA Hospital as part-time consultant. Commercial instruments were not yet readily available, so she had to design, build, and calibrate radiation detection equipment on her own. She installed it on her own, in the space set aside for her—formerly the janitor's closet—while teaching full-time at Hunter and managing the kosher household Aaron wanted.

Then, with Roswit and others, she planned and carried out experiments for the safe use of radioisotopes in humans. Her Hunter students were kept fully abreast of the work and were thrilled by it—state-of-the-art research, done by a woman hardly older than themselves. By 1950 she knew she was committed to biomedical investigation, and resigned from Hunter.

Although the VA had thought of radioisotopes as an inexpensive replacement for radium in the treatment of cancer, a book by George de Hevesy (Nobel laureate in 1943) claimed they could best be used for understanding human physiology. It was a subject Yalow knew nothing about, and she began reading up on it, realizing as she read that she would need a partner, someone skilled in internal medicine. This partner would learn physics from her, while she in turn would learn medicine. When she discussed the matter with Dr. Bernard Straus, head of medicine at the VA Hospital, he sent her a new resident, Solomon Berson, the best resident he'd ever had.

It was the start of an alliance that lasted twenty-two years, a working partnership as well as a friendship—challenging, enriching, ultimately altering the course of Dr. Yalow's life. "The thing that was particular about Sol was, he was so terribly bright." A "generalist," she calls him, trained in internal medicine, and at the same time a virtuoso violinist, a dazzling chess player, sensitive to art, literature, history, mathematics. Hard-driving and aggressive, he was a true "Type A," the term used by cardiologists to describe strivers, overachievers, those most likely to succumb to a heart attack. Although he was warm, charming, and blessed with fine-featured good looks, Berson had other, more troubling qualities, such as a certain high-handedness. According to Yalow, "I'd say you either loved him or hated him."

She admired him from the start, forgiving his faults. He was, for example, something of a "male chauvinist pig," so she deferred to him, allowing him to take the spotlight and go first, "because Sol was certainly worthy of being first in anybody's world. He was a leader in whatever he did, and it would have been very upsetting to him if I did not defer. And really," she adds, "there was nothing to lose." Why not let him go first since it mattered to him?

Their earliest experiments together explored the use of radioactive iodine in the diagnosis and treatment of thyroid disease. Later they measured blood volume by "tagging" red blood cells with radioisotopes of phosphorus or potassium—injecting them, and taking blood samples a few minutes later, on which they used a Geiger counter to monitor radioactivity.

In those first years Yalow and Berson created a kind of hybrid language between them, half medicine, half physics. They learned to think in tandem, in time developing a collaboration so close that it suggested mental telepathy. Above all, they complemented each other. According to Bernard Straus, "Berson was something of a romantic. Dr. Yalow was keen and scientific, and certainly a steadying influence. I like to say that she has an immaculate perception. She sees things steady, and she sees them whole."

If there were potential problems, she preferred to overlook them. When they began writing scientific papers together, Berson edited and polished what Yalow wrote, and in later years wrote or rewrote many of her speeches. Yet, if she changed what he wrote, he found that intolerable.

Details, she thought. Trivialities. Trivial things didn't matter to her, because she refused to let them matter.

Ever since she came to the VA, Ros Yalow had been waiting for the time when her employers would consider her irreplaceable. She wanted to start a family, but she did not want to be told to leave work at such and such a month. She became pregnant, and continued in the lab despite a VA rule against working past the fifth month. Although everyone else in the lab was aware of her pregnancy, they, too, ignored the rule. "They needed me," she explains. "I purposely waited until they did."

She remained at work until the day her son Benjamin was born, and was back in little over a week. Because she believed that every mother deserves to nurse her firstborn, she nursed Benjie for more than two months. He slept much of the day, with the result that he stayed awake most of the night. How did she manage? She slept in spurts, she says, something she'd learned to do while carrying out experiments for her doctorate. Like Benjie, they had to be tended on a round-the-clock basis.

Now that they were parents the Yalows bought a house, a small red-brick Tudor in Riverdale, a prosperous Bronx neighborhood not far from where her parents lived. They soon had a second child, Elanna. There was live-in help at home for some years, and the children's grandmother, Clara Sussman, came by every afternoon to help out. When Ros returned from work she would drive her mother home, listening to complaints that "No self-respecting mother leaves her children. . . ." But in time these complaints were forgotten, perhaps because Ros threw herself into mothering with the same intensity she brought to her work.

She came home every day for lunch, for as long as Elanna was in grade school. She took the children to the lab on weekends, where they played with the lab animals. She was the one mother in the neighborhood who could always be counted on for field trips. Once, when one of their schoolmates slept over, she learned by accident that the child had never been taught his multiplication tables, so she taught him that night. And all the while she was working sixty to eighty hours a week, sometimes a hundred hours.

Aaron helped with the children; he was now a physics professor at Cooper Union, and he shared fully in their lives and interests, taking them to the zoo, to museums, not because he'd made any kind of contract with his wife, but because he wanted to do it, just as he wanted her to work. "He wouldn't have had it otherwise," according to Ros. And once the live-in help was replaced by part-time, she did the shopping, the cooking, the serving of breakfast and dinner, because she wouldn't have had it otherwise. "If a husband feels like doing things it's fine, but I think that running a house is a wife's responsibility." What is a husband's responsibility? "I think a husband's responsibility is not to run a house," she says, with the quick smile that forestalls further questions.

She was at one and the same time thoroughly unconventional—already more successful than her husband, for one thing—and ready to defer to her male colleague, while taking full charge of a traditional household. Straddling two worlds, she was well aware of the contradiction.

About a year or so after he joined her at the hospital, Berson had said to Yalow, "Stick with me and I'll have your name up in lights." It was a remark lightly made and taken as such. But now something turned up in the lab, something unexpected, that they stumbled across in the course of their work during those years when her babies were being born. And it seemed to give weight to Berson's casual remark.

They had been using radioactive iodine to tag certain hormones and proteins, in order to study the body's methods of making and destroying those substances. One was insulin, which is made in the pancreas and required by the body to process sugar. Until then it was believed that the high levels of sugar in the blood of adult diabetics were due to insulin deficiency, for which they took injections of insulin made from the pancreases of cattle or sheep.

When a colleague suggested that a certain liver enzyme in adult diabetics might act to destroy their natural insulin, Yalow and Berson wanted to see if he was right. They injected volunteers, themselves included, with animal insulin that had been radioactively tagged. They expected that this insulin would disappear rapidly—attacked by the liver enzyme—from the systems of those test subjects who were diabetic.

But they found the opposite to be true. Adult diabetics retained their insulin *longer* than healthy volunteers. Why?

Berson and Yalow sat at desks that faced each other; this was their usual way of working. They would come into the room and argue, bouncing ideas off one another, then run to the lab to test whatever hypothesis emerged—lab coats flying as they went, still talking, in the private language they had evolved. The concept that came to them now was so much a product of this interaction that Yalow no longer remembers who first came up with it.

If adult diabetics held on to their insulin longer, it must be because their immune systems were producing antibodies to it—to the "foreign," animal insulin they'd been taking for years in therapeutic doses.

Concentrations of these suspected antibodies would be low, so low that they could never have been detected with conventional means. But the Yalow-Berson team used their highly sensitive radioisotope measurements and saw they were right. There were antibodies.

This discovery was in no way earthshaking, but it was new and valuable, and they wrote a paper about it, unaware that the scientific world believed the insulin molecule too small to create antibodies. The paper was then sent to *"Science,"* but rejected. It went next to *The Journal of Clinical Investigation,* and was again rejected. "Interesting and praiseworthy," the editor noted, but unsuitable for publication—the writing was incoherent, he said, and experts in the field emphatically denied their conclusion that an insulin antibody could be responsible for retention of insulin.

They rewrote the paper, resubmitted, and were again rejected. It was rewritten once more with added documentation, the offending words "insulin antibody" removed from the title, and finally published in 1956.

What they had done up to that point seemed to affect only research into diabetes. Yet it had implications that reached far beyond a single disease. "In studying the reaction of insulin with antibodies," as Dr. Yalow later wrote, "we appreciated that we had developed a tool with the potential for measuring circulating insulin." Moreover they came to realize that this same process made it possible to measure *virtually any substance created in the human body,* because almost any substance can be made to produce antibodies. Some would have to be treated chemically to trigger the immune reaction, but this, too, was possible.

They named their discovery radio-immuno-assay, RIA, meaning a radioactive tool, using immunologic methods to measure (assay) chemical or biological substances.

Radioimmunoassay has been described in the following way, by the Swedish Professor Rolf Luft when introducing Dr. Yalow at the Nobel prize ceremony: "As a result of mixing in a test tube a known quantity of radioactive insulin with a known quantity of antibodies against insulin, a specific amount of the insulin becomes attached to these antibodies. Subsequently, if one adds to this mixture a small amount of blood which contains insulin, the insulin of the blood becomes similarly attached to the antibodies and a certain portion of the radioactive insulin is detached from the antibodies. The higher the concentration of insulin is in the blood sample, the larger is the amount of radioactive insulin that will be detached. . . . The amount of radioactive insulin thus removed can easily be determined, providing an exact measure of the amount of insulin present in the blood sample."

Dr. Luft adds that the technique can be called "genial in all its simplicity." At the same time, such is its sensitivity that it can detect the presence of a sugar cube dissolved in Lake Erie.

RIA was presented to the world in 1959, three years after publication of the paper on insulin antibodies. During that time Berson and Yalow had worked "day and night at ninety miles an hour," as a colleague recalled—until midnight, past midnight, into the hours before dawn when all the others had crept home. Yet both were unfailingly at their desks by seven or eight next morning. Berson, the romantic, provided the biological brilliance, while Yalow's contribution was the mathematical sinew and bone, the physical underpinning that held them to earth.

They then became a public-relations team. "We not only discovered radioimmunoassay, we had to popularize it," Yalow explains. They traveled tirelessly. It became a habit with her, one that continues into her late sixties. "You don't go to the West Coast for two days and come back on the red-eye unless you're crazy like me," she says. Sometimes they went separately, more often together, and she never knew if people did or didn't talk; she felt free to do as she saw fit.

The "cheerful little dark-haired person, not very imposing," had matured, and with maturity she had taken on muscle. People claimed she was overly aggressive. So was Berson, for that matter. One of their colleagues speculated that the honors and recognition that seemed slow in coming might have been awarded more quickly if the two of them together hadn't been seen as a pair of blazing guns.

But aggressiveness can be forgiven in a man. With Yalow it seemed out of place. She was "hard to take," people said, stubborn, impatient, and overbearing. Her lab staff saw her in a different light—as the woman who told them to wear their galoshes when it snowed, who brewed the coffee for their meetings, and prepared at home all the food for lab parties, bringing it in, laying it out, making sure everyone ate. She'd never minded deferring to Berson any more than she minded running a kosher household for Aaron, and the lab staff and the younger colleagues were her professional family. Why not make their coffee? Why not discuss their personal problems when they wanted a motherly listener?

As for Aaron, the long hours, the travel, and prolonged absences in no way disturbed him. He was proud of the success his wife had had so far and hoped she'd go on to still greater success. If she outshone him—well, in most cases one of two spouses outshone the other; why shouldn't it be the wife?

Throughout the 1960s work in the lab continued in high gear. RIA techniques were used in endocrinology, in virology—there seemed no end to the secrets it could unlock, and by the end of the decade everyone was doing radioimmunoassay work, on several continents. Entire issues of learned journals were devoted to it.

In 1968 Sol Berson was offered a position as chairman of medicine at the new Mt. Sinai Hospital. Yalow didn't think too highly of that. "I had the conviction" she said, "that this was the place from which our fame came. There was nothing to be gained by being a professor. . . ."

The importance of RIA was now fully established; from other labs they heard news of RIAs to study infertility, steroid production, to screen blood banks for hepatitis virus, to test for abuse of heroin, methadone. They were winning awards. They belonged to prestigious scientific societies. On rare occasions, and only between themselves, they even mentioned "The Big One," meaning the Nobel Prize, "but it wasn't really for real because . . . you know, we came from a little-known institution. We knew our work was very good, but—"

However, Berson had a family, and the new position paid a salary two-and-a-half times what the VA paid. He'd still come to the lab, he said, after work in the evenings, as often as possible.

Other things were changing as well. Not so long ago the Yalow children had been happy to tour the Western States with their parents, visiting all the national parks, something they did at a fairly rapid clip, with Ros driving. "You didn't have 55 miles an hour then," she remarks. Other summers they went to Europe or Israel, never extravagantly, always with one or both children. Now, at fourteen, Elanna was in the midst of an adolescent crisis.

"I rejected the house. I didn't wear nice clothes as she wanted me to," Elanna said later, and "I wasn't interested in science."

Benjamin was less openly rebellious. He had always been intrigued by science in general, by computers in particular, but there was nothing of the workaholic in him. "My mother's wish for me" he said, "is to . . . move rapidly up the ranks. But I just don't think that's fun. I just don't have that drive or ambition." Perhaps Elanna spoke for both of them when she said, in her mid-twenties, that they had seen the price their mother paid for reaching the peaks—the long hours of absence during their early childhood—and decided the price was too high, that she had missed out on too much.

Simon Sussman had died some years earlier. Most of the Bronx suffered desperately from poverty, crime, and drugs. Riverdale remained serene, but to drive even a few blocks away meant entering a battlefield. Yet other things had stayed the same. Clara Sussman was alive and flourishing and tremendously proud of her daughter, as were the aunts. Sol Berson came back to the lab one evening each week.

Then, in April of 1972, he died of a heart attack at the age of fifty-four. Yalow had lost a close friend, an admired partner, perhaps for a time her equilibrium. She thought briefly of going to medical school. She asked that the lab be called the Solomon A. Berson Research Laboratory so that his name would be on all papers produced there. She was depressed, uncertain—not only a woman in a man's world but the only physicist among physicians. Many people were sure she was finished, that she'd never do a thing but putter around the lab. They thought Berson had been the brains while she was only the motor. According to a young colleague, "People at the highest levels of science said this; even people who had actually worked with her. Berson himself had known better. . . ."

Equipment for doing RIA tests was now earning many millions of dollars annually for drug companies. Neither Berson nor Yalow had thought of patenting their process, perhaps because they never foresaw its turning into a gold mine, more likely because their minds just didn't work that way. And the possibility of becoming a spokesperson for one or another of these drug companies did not appeal to Yalow now. She'd be unable to speak her mind if paid by drug companies, and besides, money was never one of her goals. What she longed for was "The Big One."

The Nobel Prize is never given posthumously, and no survivor of a scientific team had ever won, let alone a woman perceived by some as the secondary partner. Furthermore, a voting member of the Nobel Committee had already said her chances were finished, and she knew he'd said it.

Meanwhile, she was joined by a young collaborator, Eugene Straus, the son of the Bernard Straus who first brought her together with Berson. There was work to be done, enormous amounts of it because Berson had made many commitments she now had to fulfill—and after that she meant to show the world she was more than the secondary partner.

In the next four years Yalow published some sixty papers and won a dozen medical awards. In 1976 she received the prestigious Albert Lasker Prize for Basic Medical Research, the first woman so honored. Perhaps "The Big One" would follow—this was often the case, first the Lasker, then the Nobel, and when it failed to happen Aaron said she wasn't discouraged. "Her reaction was just, 'What do I have to do to win?'"

The year 1977 was the same; during the early hours of October 14 neither of them slept well. Aaron got up at three; Ros was up at three-thirty. She went back to bed but he stayed up. At five-thirty both were up, so they turned on the radio. Nothing.

"Well okay," Ros said. "It looks like we probably have to wait till next year," and they both got dressed and ate breakfast.

She was at her desk at 6:45 when the phone call came from Stockholm. She had won half the prize, the other half being shared by Roger Guillemin and Andrew V. Schally for work on hormones in the brain. Yalow was the second woman laureate in physiology or medicine, the first in any science to be educated entirely in the United States.

In his speech at the prize-giving ceremony, Dr. Luft spoke of a "revolution in the field of hormonal research, a field where one refers to the time period before Yalow, and the new epoch that began with her achievement. Her methodology and the modifications thereof subsequently made their triumphant journey far beyond her own field of research, reaching into vast territories of biology and medicine. It has been said that Yalow changed the life of a multitude of researchers. . . . *Rarely have so many had so few to thank for so much.*"

———————

Some Nobelists claim the award is a burden, that it brings too many requests for lectures, interviews, public appearances. But Yalow made a copy of the Nobel medal and wore it on a chain around her neck, surely the only laureate ever to do so, and she never complained; she rarely refused demands on her time. "It should happen to everyone," she said.

And she glowed. Her smiling face appeared in newspapers and magazines both well known and obscure. Under such headlines as "She Cooks, She Cleans, She Wins the

Rosalyn Yalow—scientist and devoted wife and mother. Here, she is shown with her mother, Clara Sussman and her daughter, Elanna.

Nobel Prize," Yalow offered opinions on the status of women, on parenting, marriage, nuclear energy, and the exaggerated fears of radiation. She posed for photographers with Benjamin and the new word processor he was teaching her to use; with Elanna and Clara Sussman; with Aaron seated at the dining table as she served him breakfast. In each of these pictures her features have taken on softness and fullness; she seems relaxed, warm, even bubbly.

She told *Family Health,* "Once you've become a Nobel

prizewinner, you're so special. . . . I could probably do anything, even something silly, because a Nobel prizewinner can do no wrong." She told *Newsweek,* "Before Nobel, nobody had heard of me. Now I'm much more in the public eye, and I can do things I've never done before."

Had she ever, in her adult life, done "somthing silly"? Perhaps not, and after a time she would revert to type, becoming once again brisk, guarded, incapable of silliness. But for awhile she allowed herself the luxury of feeling light-headed, of being bowled over by the length of the journey she'd made from the walkup apartments and dollar dresses of the Bronx, to Stockholm, the Concert Hall, the gold medal given by the young king.

One thing she did refuse was more money. VA salaries, even hers, were comparatively modest, but she had no interest in going elsewhere. "As a matter of principle I have always turned down more money than I could spend usefully. Too much money is disruptive. . . ."

There was another refusal. In June of 1978 Yalow wrote a letter to the *Ladies' Home Journal,* declining one of their Woman of the Year awards. She wanted to see men and women competing on equal terms, she said, and was not pleased to be told her achievements were remarkable for a woman.

The VA Medical Center stands behind cyclone fencing in a rundown section of the rundown Bronx, much of it a free-fire zone where police go only in pairs, and the streets belong to armed gangs and drug dealers.

Dr. Yalow still comes here to the lab six days a week. Slightly overweight, carefully made up, her hair cosmeti-

Dr. Yalow at work in her laboratory at the Bronx VA Medical Center.

cally darkened, she wears dangling gold earrings, the replica of the Nobel medal, and a starchy white coat. Although her lab has long since outgrown the janitor's closet, it is comparatively modest in scale. "I have never aspired to . . . a laboratory or a cadre of investigators-in-training that is more extensive than I can personally interact with," she says.

Young scientists come to her for training from China, Uganda, India, Japan, and she is immensely proud of the fact that all "foreign people who have trained in my laboratory have returned home," where they contribute to health care in Third World countries. She considers them her professional children.

Aaron is retired now, after a long, satisfying career as a physics professor. Elanna, with a husband and new baby, a doctorate from Stanford in educational psychology, and an MBA, has recently begun work for a firm engaged in setting up daycare centers. Benjamin manages the central computer system for the City University of New York, which includes nine senior colleges, Hunter among them.

In two or so years Dr. Yalow expects to close up the lab. Then she plans to start a new career, becoming involved in public affairs and education. "I think I have a real social responsibility to interact with the community on an educational basis. I think our country is confronted by what I call a phobic fear of radiation. They need an education, and I'm prepared to give it to them . . . if they'll listen. I have a certain amount of credibility as a scientist. I've been very careful not to be involved with money from the nuclear power industry, or the pharmaceutical industry. I come with clean hands."

She has never regretted not having patented RIA, never regretted not being rich. "What do I need money for?" she asks. "I can't think of anything I want. I wasn't handed college or graduate school or anything else on a silver platter. I had to work very hard, but I did it because I wanted to. That's the real key to happiness. I think unhappy people are those who feel that circumstances are forcing them into a pattern. Happy people are not slaves to the system. . . . Nobody's ever been able to tell me what to do."

———————

Barbara McClintock

CHAPTER 3

BARBARA McCLINTOCK:

1983 Nobel Prize for Medicine

"THE GENES THAT JUMP"

A woman walked up to the side entrance of a building in the Agricultural School and tried the door. This being Sunday morning, the door was locked. She gave the door a good kick; then she rummaged through the pockets of her trousers in search of the key she already knew she'd forgotten, and after that she turned and circled the building, on the lookout for an open window.

When she found one she jumped for the sill, clutched it, and hoisted herself up through the opening, throwing one leg over, then the other, till she dropped from sight. None of this would have been in any way unusual if the climber had been a man. It would have seemed like a practical solution to a minor problem.

Yet it was unusual. It was so unusual, in fact, that a passerby who happened to have a camera used it to record the event from the rear—the one trousered leg followed by the other before they slid through the opening under the window sash. The time was the mid-1930s, when a woman professor was expected to dress like a lady and conduct herself like a lady.

This particular woman professor spent much of her working life in a cornfield, where skirts got in her way. Therefore, she chose to ignore convention by wearing trousers, man-tailored shirts, and flat, sturdy shoes—even here, at the University of Missouri in Columbia, Missouri, a highly conventional place.

The passerby who snapped the picture showed it to others. Some laughed, some clicked their tongues in disapproval. Many years later it was shown to the woman herself, Barbara McClintock, but that was long after she'd left Columbia, Missouri, long after she'd given up hope of fitting herself into what she saw as the straitjacket role of woman professor.

If childhood can be thought of as a country, Barbara McClintock's was a land of contrasts, where broad, sunny meadows alternated with patches of dense forest, hidden from the sun.

She was born in 1902, in Hartford, Connecticut, the third of four children of Thomas Henry McClintock, a physician, and his wife, Sara. They had married in their early twenties, despite the disapproval of Sara's father, and their babies came in quick succession. Marjorie was born within a year, Mignon two years later, Barbara two years after Mignon, so that Sara had three little girls within the space of five years—and a husband recently out of medical school. She was utterly unprepared for the hardships she had to face. She had been brought up in comfort, an attractive and talented young woman, a musician, poet, and painter. Now she struggled with debts, and the babies.

Nothing was to be expected from Sara's father since he disapproved of her marriage, so she gave piano lessons, and used her own small inheritance to pay off some of the medical-school debts. At least she had help from her husband with the babies. He was good with babies. "My father should have been a pediatrician," Barbara McClintock said later, "because he was very perceptive with children."

He had wanted a son, and when this third daughter appeared he dealt with his disappointment by raising her like a son, buying her boxing gloves when she was four, and later the toys and games usually given to boys. According to family legend, Barbara was always her father's favorite.

But her mother had been under tremendous pressure when Barbara was born, and relations between the two were apparently troubled from the start. A year-and-a-half later there was another child, this time the longed-for son, and Mrs. McClintock's resources were strained to the limit. Both mother and daughter suffered, each in her own way, during this period, until it must have seemed that the only solution was to send the little girl away for a time.

She was about three years old when she went to live with an aunt and uncle in Massachusetts, remaining with them off and on for several years. Barbara remembered her uncle as "a great big man with a great big voice," a fish dealer whose truck seemed to be forever breaking down. She believed her early interest in cars dated from those times when she watched his gallant struggles with the truck.

In later years Barbara McClintock claimed she had "absolutely not" been homesick when living with her uncle. She loved the country freedom, she said. "I enjoyed myself immensely."

Meanwhile her parents had moved to Flatbush, a semi-rural neighborhood in Brooklyn, and Barbara came home for good when she was ready to start school. However, her relations with her mother were as difficult, if not worse, than before. She wanted nothing to do with her mother.

When her mother tried to embrace her, Barbara cried out, "No!" She enjoyed being alone. She was "thinking about things," she said. Some mysterious and painful difference in their personalities had placed a barrier between mother and daughter, and according to family legend Barbara's childhood was independent, self-sufficient, and solitary.

Her mother found this craving for solitude alarming. Surely she must have wondered where she herself had failed. Yet both parents were affectionate as well as conscientious. They wanted their children to live joyfully and without constraint, believing childhood ought to be a time for freedom. Rules, discipline, and seriousness could wait until adolescence. In fact, their ideas about childraising were in some ways ahead of their time.

Barbara's father, for example, told the grade school his children attended that they were not to be given homework. If one of them didn't feel like going to school they could stay home, even for months at a time. When Barbara showed an interest in ice-skating her parents bought her "the very best shoe and skate outfit that they could get for me. Every good day for skating, I was out skating at Prospect Park rather than going to school." After school, when her brother and his friends came home, she played street games with them. She wanted bloomers to match her dresses, in order to move as freely as the boys, and this, too, her parents supplied. According to Marjorie, they took no interest in what their children *should* be, only in what they were.

And Barbara was a loner, a rough-and-tumble tomboy, with an intensely sensitive nature that her parents respected. She remembered how one of the neighbor women saw her playing basketball or volleyball on the street "and called me to her house, and . . . invited me in, stating that it was time that I learned to do the things that girls should be doing. I stood there and looked at her. I didn't say anything, but I turned around and went directly home, and told my mother what had happened. My mother went directly to the telephone and told that woman, 'Don't ever do that again!' "

These ideas about freedom and individualism were not the special invention of Dr. and Mrs. McClintock, but rather part of a philosophy then current in certain educated circles. Many believed in home schooling; Thomas Hunt Morgan, the pioneer geneticist Barbara was to meet later in life, kept his daughters at home, to be taught by their mother until third grade. Compulsory schooling was thought to deprive the young child of fresh air and the closeness to nature that were more important than lessons.

After grade school, the McClintock children went on to Erasmus Hall High School. Here Barbara's enthusiasm for football, baseball, and tree-climbing gave way to a hunger for learning. She loved science, and she loved problem-solving. "It was a tremendous joy, the whole process of finding that answer. Just pure joy," she said.

This was not at all what her parents had been led to expect. The carefree childhood was supposed to be followed by an adolescence in which boys became manly and girls became womanly, each sex taking on the tasks society required it to accomplish. Barbara's two older sisters were excellent students; Marjorie even won a scholarship to Vassar, but her mother believed a college-educated woman was less likely to find a husband, and talked her out of Vassar. Instead, she became a professional musician. Mignon became an actress for a time. Later both sisters married.

Barbara, on the other hand, was not persuaded by her

mother, nor was she alarmed by her mother's fears that she might turn into a college professor, "a strange person, a person that didn't belong to society."

But she was different, and knew she was different. She was still a loner in her teenage years as she had been in childhood. She showed no interest in boys except as fellow-athletes. She cared nothing about her appearance, and she had intellectual leanings.

During high school she tried to come to grips with this differentness. "I found that handling it in a way that other people would not appreciate, because it was not the standard conduct, might cause me great pain, but I would take the consequences. . . . And I would do that regardless of the pain . . . as a decision that it was the only way that I could keep my sanity."

When America entered the first World War Dr. McClintock was sent overseas as a military surgeon, leaving his wife in charge of the family. The two younger children proved to be more than she could manage. The only son ran off to sea, as his great-grandfather had done, while Barbara persisted in her desire for higher education. There was no money and her mother was by now actively opposed to college. But Barbara promised herself that one day she would go to Cornell and study science. Cornell was one of the few universities committed to the training of women in science, and its College of Agriculture had no tuition fees.

After graduating from Erasmus at the age of sixteen she went to work at an employment agency, and spent all her free time in the library. "I was going to get the equivalent of a college education," she said, "if I had to do it on my own."

Then her father returned from the army. He must have taken Barbara's side in the argument, because her mother's opposition seemed to melt away overnight. Barbara rushed to Ithaca, New York, by train, and at eight the next morning stood on line to register for the fall term at Cornell. "I was entranced at the very first lecture I went to. It was zoology, and I was just completely entranced. I was doing now what I really wanted to do, and I never lost that joy all through college."

A photo of her during her college years shows Barbara seated on a garden chair, smiling a broad, dimpled smile. A cigarette dangles from her fingers, she seems impish, mischievous, a pretty girl caught in the act of discovering life. For a surprising transformation had taken place at Cornell. It was as if Barbara had burst out of her cocoon and become a social being, aware of others, reaching out to others, for the first time enjoying the company of others.

"There were many things that one learned in college that one could not ordinarily learn then outside," she said later. "You met people from all kinds of groups and societies; you were able to gain knowledge from people from different places, with different backgrounds."

People responded to her interest in them. She was elected president of the women's freshman class, and was rushed by a sorority. But when she realized the effect of the sorority system—the hurt inflicted on those girls who were deemed unacceptable—she refused to join, because "I just couldn't stand that kind of discrimination." She chose to remain in a dormitory, with a tight little group of women, none of them scientists.

She took up banjo, and later on played tenor banjo with a jazz improvisation group. One day she had a long talk with the local barber, and persuaded him to cut off her hair—the first girl at Cornell to be "shingled." This created a sensation all over the campus.

And her family basked in the sunshine of her visits home, amazed and delighted with this popular, outgoing Barbara, who seemed no longer in danger of becoming a strange person. There were even men in her life now.

She went out with a number of men, including several to whom she felt "a very strong emotional attachment," usually artists of one kind or another. But with the end of her second year as a coed, some sort of self-questioning apparently took place. Barbara McClintock was so reticent about her personal life that this process can only be guessed at, but it seems clear that she had been thinking over her relationships with men, and trying to decide what part they would play in her life. The answer was that the old Barbara, the childhood loner, was her real self, that men, romance, and marriage were not for her.

Perhaps there was one single event, one man, whose appeal to her sexual nature was so frightening to her that she retreated forever from men and sex. It is equally possible that this change of heart had nothing or little to do with men, and that it wasn't sex she feared, but rather intimacy with anyone. Friends can be pushed away, but a lover or husband is always there, always on intimate terms, and there are people whom Nature has not designed for intimacy with others.

In any case she finally saw that with "any man I met, nothing could have lasted. I was not adjusted, never had been, to being closely associated with anybody, even members of my own family. . . . There was not that strong necessity for a personal attachment to anybody. I just didn't feel it." She said this years later, when she was almost 80. "And I could never understand marriage. I really do not even now. . . . I never went through the experience of requiring it."

By the end of her junior year she had decided that she would spend the rest of her life alone, as a working scientist. And in 1983, when the Nobel Prize Committee asked for a brief autobiography, she began hers with the following: "In the fall of 1921 I attended the only course in genetics open to undergraduate students at Cornell University." It was as if parents and childhood never existed, as if she sprang into being for the first time when entering that class in genetics.

Genetics—the science of heredity—was a new discipline, only two years older than McClintock herself. Modern genetics is said to have started in 1900, with the rediscovery of studies done decades earlier by an Austrian monk, Gregor Mendel. Cultivating peas in the monastery garden, he observed the results of cross-fertilization and worked out the laws of inherited characteristics. The first is the law of segregation, which has three parts: hereditary factors (now called genes) occur in pairs; the two factors in a pair separate during the division of sex cells, each sperm or egg receiving only one member of the pair; and each factor in a pair will be present in half the sperms or eggs.

Mendel's second law, the law of independent assortment, states that each pair of factors is inherited independently of all other pairs. Scientists have since learned that this applies only to genes on different chromosomes (the thread-like structure that contains the genetic material); others that are linked, or on the same chromosome, tend to be inherited together.

Although Mendel's work was meticulously done, when he published it in 1866 its importance went unrecognized. Chromosomes were unknown at the time, as were genes; moreover Mendel was unknown, a monk rather than an established scientist, and his paper simply sank from sight.

But the latter years of the nineteenth century brought rapid development in cytology, the study of cells. Chromosomes and the gene material were discovered. Mendel was republished. It was suggested that Mendel's "factors" were related to chromosomal structures. Thomas Hunt Morgan, working with fruit flies (Drosophila) at Columbia University, did a series of studies from which he concluded that genes were strung on the chromosomes like beads, each gene controlling a specific trait of the fruit fly.

Many scientists resisted Morgan's conclusions. European visitors to his "Fly Room" at Columbia were chiefly impressed by the filth of the place, where thousands of red-eyed flies were kept in milk bottles and fed on mashed bananas. But Drosophila proved to be a highly useful tool in genetic research, because they complete their life cycle in about two weeks, and also because they are subject to a large number of readily detectable genetic variations. This enables researchers to trace hereditary characteristics through many generations in a short period of time.

Much of our modern knowledge of genetics stems ultimately from Morgan's pioneering experiments in that evil-smelling Fly Room. At Cornell, however, there were no fruit flies. Cornell did its genetics with corn, not the yellow corn found at the supermarket, but the wild form known as maize, with blue, brown, or red kernels. These richly colored kernels—each one the result of a unique mating event—provide visible evidence of genetic changes from one generation to the next, and they are lovely to look at. In the 1980s, on those rare occasions when Barbara McClintock agreed to be interviewed and photographed, she was never without an ear of corn, which she held much as a musician would hold a beloved instrument.

After graduation in 1923 she wanted to continue work in genetics, but Cornell's plant-breeding department, where genetics was taught, did not take women on the graduate level. She went into botany instead, and in the course of her first year made a major discovery.

She found she could identify individual maize chromosomes under the microscope, each of the 10 chromosomes having a distinctive shape and structure. "I had it done within two or three days—the whole thing done, clear, sharp, and nice." People had been looking in the wrong place, she explained; she looked in the right place, at a different stage in the development of the plant.

Now for the first time it was possible to identify which chromosome carried the genes for a particular trait, and to study chromosomes and traits together. Few graduate students begin their careers with such a flourish. She wrote her doctoral thesis on it, received her Ph.D. in 1927, and stayed at Cornell as an instructor in botany while continuing to explore the implications of her discovery.

The period that followed—1928 to 1935—became known as the Golden Age of maize cytogenetics (cytology combined with genetics). For McClintock, too, it was a golden age. She loved every aspect of the work—the spring planting, the frenzied time of fertilization, the harvest, when the papery wrapping of the maize husk was torn away to reveal the mature ear in all its varied colors and patterns. When not in the cornfield she was in her laboratory, bent over a microscope. To some, this was drudgery, a task to be passed on to assistants, but to McClintock it was problem-solving, and it never ceased to bring her joy.

During this time she had the companionship of two graduate students—George Beadle (Nobel laureate in 1958) and Marcus Rhoades, who became her lifelong friends. Others joined their group from time to time, but these three were the core of it, comrades, sharers of ideas that excited them. A picture taken in 1929 shows four tall, rangy men— bags strapped inside their belts for collecting corn tassels and ear-shoots—and one very small woman, who stands a little apart from the rest. She has on knee-socks and knee-length knickers, she appears to weigh about 90 pounds, and her hair is short and rumpled, like a schoolboy's. According to Marcus Rhoades, "She was the dominant figure in the talented Cornell group . . . and she, more than anyone else, was responsible for a long series of remarkable findings."

The summer of 1929 brought another lifelong friend, Harriet Creighton, a lively, athletic 20-year-old, ready to start graduate work at Cornell. Creighton became McClintock's apprentice. They spent much of their leisure time together, playing strenuous tennis every day at five o'clock, or going on long drives with Creighton at the wheel—she was known as a daredevil driver.

They enjoyed one another's company. According to Creighton, McClintock had a great sense of humor, and a sense of mischief as well. She remembers no particular jokes, only that the older woman saw "the ludicrousness of many a situation." Others recalled her hearty laughter and her habit of slapping her knees when she laughed.

In the laboratory, Harriet Creighton had to learn to follow McClintock's explanations, and this was not easy. McClintock had a style peculiarly her own; it was close-packed, at times cryptic, with abrupt transitions from one line of thought to the next. Many found it tough going.

In time Creighton was ready to start on her doctoral research, under McClintock's supervision. They proposed to prove—once and for all, conclusively—that chromosomes really do carry genetic information as Mendel's experiments indicated. This would be done by showing that the physical exchange between chromosomes, which occurs in the early stages of cell division for reproduction, is accompanied by an exchange of genetic material.

Creighton was in no great hurry to finish the work; she hardly realized its importance at the start, nor did she know that a German investigator, a *Drosophila* man, was moving along similar lines. He would have published first, except for the intervention of Thomas Hunt Morgan, who paid a visit to Cornell in 1931.

Six feet tall, bearded, with eyes of a startling blue, his hair uncombed, his trousers usually held up by a string, Morgan was then in his middle sixties and one of the great men of his generation. He had a Southern accent, a Southerner's easy charm when he wanted to put it on, many eccentricities, and great kindness of heart.

Morgan went round the Cornell laboratories to see what people were doing. When he came to Creighton she explained the project; he asked if it had been written up, but she said they had barely begun.

Morgan told her they had plenty of evidence already. Then and there he wrote a letter to the editor of *Proceedings of the National Academy of Science,* telling him to expect the Creighton-McClintock paper within two weeks. It was published in August of 1941, and has been called the cornerstone of experimental genetics.

Morgan is supposed to have said later, "I thought it was about time that corn got a chance to beat *Drosophila!*" But Marcus Rhoades could never believe this account. He said it didn't sound at all like Morgan to take pleasure in jumping the gun on another scientist.

Between 1929 and 1931 McClintock published nine papers of major importance, but she was still only an instructor, without tenure, without a definite future. Cornell had no women professors in any field except home economics, nor was such an appointment made till the late 1940s. She was afraid that if she stayed on indefinitely she would become an embarrassment both to Cornell and herself.

For the next two years she divided her time among three institutions—the University of Missouri at Columbia; California Institute of Technology (CalTech) at Pasadena; and Cornell, where her cornfield was. Cornell and the cornfield were home to her. She visited her parents and sisters, and was especially fond of her sister Marjorie, but their homes were never "home" to her.

At Missouri, with her friend and former colleague Lewis Stadler, she studied X-ray induced mutations, or changes, in maize chromosomes. She found circular, or ring, chromosomes, which often produced mixed-color maize kernels, a discovery that was to be vital to her later work.

Then she went on to CalTech at the invitation of Thomas Hunt Morgan, who had gone there in 1928 to set up a genetics department. The Morgans lived in a beautiful old ranch house, filled with elegant mahogany furniture they had brought from New York. There were big sunny rooms, a player piano, a full-size billiard table, a patio. Visitors came and went, including the Morgans' grown children, and McClintock settled in comfortably for the winter. Morgan's wife, Lilian, had a gift for making young people comfortable.

Lilian Morgan was a scientist as well. She held a master's degree in biology, and had worked in her husband's Columbia University laboratory, in an outer room, a kind of second circle beyond which the women workers never penetrated. Her work was unpaid, she had no real place in the laboratory, yet she made discoveries of genuine value to *Drosophila* genetics.

This was the fate of many women scientists—the second circle, the devotion to a husband's career. What paths were open to women who did not marry fellow-scientists, and who consequently had no labs in which their presence would be tolerated? It was a question McClintock must have asked herself many times during the course of that winter. She didn't care about money or what it could buy. Clothes, for example, never mattered to her; she said she had no interest in what she called "decorating the torso." What interested her was a cornfield, a laboratory, a place to live, and enough money to hold body and soul together—but where? The women's colleges had jobs for women—Harriet Creighton made her career at a women's college—but they did no research.

During this two-year period McClintock was suported by a National Research Council fellowship, and she'd been having a wonderful time. "I was so interested in what I was doing I could hardly wait to get up in the morning and get at it." But what would she do after that?

The Rockefeller Foundation offered her a two-year research position in the genetics laboratory at Cornell. This offer was made at the urgent request of Morgan and others, Morgan insisting she was "definitely the best person in the world" in the cytology of maize genetics. But he also spoke of her "personality difficulties," saying she was "sore at the world because of her conviction that she would have a much freer scientific opportunity if she were a man."

Cornell had been reluctant to have her back, partly, they said, because she was not too successful as a teacher of undergraduates. But they did take her. She was once more at home in Cornell, traveling a hundred miles every three days in a little Ford Model A roadster to visit her cornfields.

Meanwhile, her friends were finding permanent jobs— George Beadle on his way to Harvard, Marcus Rhoades with the Department of Agriculture—while McClintock was simply hanging on from one year to the next. A woman with an international reputation, recognized as such by most of her Cornell colleagues, she wanted only what was due to her— permanence, independence. They were nowhere in sight.

———————

In the mid-1930s Lewis Stadler was building an important genetics facility at Columbia, Missouri. He managed to get McClintock an appointment as assistant professor, although not without difficulty. It was her first offer of a faculty position, poorly paid, without tenure, but she accepted. Over the next few years she was to publish a series of papers on mutation and the repeated rounds of chromosome breakage and fusion.

But her stay at the University of Missouri was soured almost from the start. It was a small place in a very small and stodgy town. According to Lewis Stadler's son David, "They liked people they were comfortable with."

McClintock arrived in her little roadster, looking like a coed on a lark. To David Stadler, then a 10-year-old, she seemed lively, vivacious, "a glamorous person, driving around in this Ford. It was so sporty. It wasn't anything like the sedans most people had." But the car and the trousers she habitually wore marked her as an outsider. So did her behavior.

She was outspoken, at times abrasive. A quick thinker, she had little patience with those who were less quick. She had been hired both to do research and to teach, but considered formal teaching a bore, an unrewarding repetition of what she already knew.

Although science professors traditionally train graduate students in their laboratories, McClintock discouraged graduate students from training with her. She preferred working alone, and in future years took considerable pride in the number of hours she spent entirely alone. She balked at calendars and fixed schedules, she never bothered to conceal her boredom with academic committees.

She had, moreover, a mystical streak in her nature, a deeply held belief in the oneness of things. This led to an interest in Tibetan Buddhism, and the conviction that many bodily processes—temperature, circulation—could be brought under the control of the mind. Most scientists are scornful of the nonrational; the term "biofeedback" was unknown at the time, and her mysticism was seen as one more peculiarity, one more example of her failure to fit in.

She knew she didn't fit. She had no intention of changing, having learned long ago that she was different and that she had to take the consequences. But she worked hard, single-mindedly, with joy and dedication, and her work was superb—she knew that, too; she never underestimated herself. And she wanted to be judged solely on the basis of her work.

Then the Dean of Liberal Arts promoted another woman to the rank of associate professor in zoology, which meant tenure, an assured future. This other woman was not a rule-breaker; neither was she in McClintock's class as a scientist.

A sense of claustrophobia settled in on her. Even the cornfield felt crowded now, without enough room for her corn. Heartsick, "brooding about myself," she decided she'd had her fill of universities, that there was no hope "for a

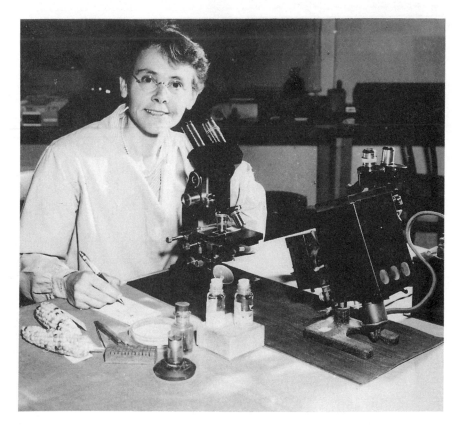

Dr. McClintock at work in the laboratory at Cold Spring Harbor, 1947. Notice the ears of corn near her hand.

maverick like me to ever be at a university." She left in 1941.

Later that year the Carnegie Institution of Washington offered McClintock an appointment in the genetics department of its Cold Spring Harbor facility. The offer included a cornfield, a laboratory, a home, as well as a salary, and they were eager to have her. McClintock was at first unsure, perhaps fearing another failure like the one at Missouri, but she accepted because there was no other place to go.

On the Sound side of Long Island, near Oyster Bay, Cold Spring Harbor was only an hour by train from Manhattan; yet it seemed worlds removed from it. There were rambling Victorian buildings, somewhat shabby, with peeling paint and patched screens. A long grassy stretch led down to the water and a sandspit for swimming. Woodsy, filled with birdsong in summer, the place attracted scores of scientists to summer research institutes. But in winter, with everyone gone, it was gray, lonely, far away from other sites of scientific activity. In the early 1940s McClintock was the only maize geneticist there.

People said that because the Cold Spring Harbor community was so small in winter, it became one big family. But McClintock felt she didn't belong to that family. Scientifically speaking there was no one to talk to. Secretaries and the men who prepared the cornfields always liked her, and she enjoyed talking to them, especially about movies they'd seen in nearby Huntington. But science was another matter. She longed for shoptalk with like-minded people. As she told Harriet Creighton, she just wasn't having any fun at Cold Spring Harbor.

But she had planted her cornfield; she had work to sustain and nourish her, work that had become the central fact of her existence. The corn was her family, her children, her trusted friend. She said once, "No two plants are exactly alike. They're all different, and as a consequence, you have to know that difference. . . . I start with the seedling, and I don't want to leave it. I don't feel I really know the story if I don't watch the plant all the way along. So I know every plant in the field. I know them intimately, and I find it a great pleasure to know them."

Plants, McClintock believes, are greatly undervalued.

We are not fully aware of their abilities: "Animals can walk around, but plants have to stay still and to do the same things, with ingenious mechanisms. . . . For instance . . . if you pinch a leaf of a plant you set off electric pulses. You can't touch a plant without setting off an electric pulse. . . . They do a lot of responding to their environment. They can do almost anything you can think of. But just because they sit there, anybody walking down the road considers them just a plastic area to look at, [as if] they're not really alive."

While observing chromosomes under her microscope, "I found that the more I worked with them the bigger and bigger [they] got, and when I was really working with them I wasn't outside, I was down there. I was part of the system. . . . It surprised me because I actually felt as if I were right down there and these were my friends."

The early years at Cold Spring Harbor were productive as well as rewarding. Honors and recognition came her way. In 1944 McClintock was named to the National Academy of Science, the third woman so honored. She was elected president of the Genetics Society of America, their first woman president. And she was on the brink of a discovery of vast importance, one with revolutionary implications. Like many such discoveries it would seem so wildly improbable that people called her "crazy, absolutely mad at times."

Other events were taking place in the field of genetics during this period; they, too, were to have revolutionary effects, and by coincidence they, too, were partly rooted in Cold Spring Harbor.

By 1930 genes were seen as beads on the string of the chromosomes, very stable, almost immune to external circumstances. The researchers who developed this view, working chiefly with *Drosophila* and maize, came to be called classical geneticists.

During the next 10 years interest shifted from maize and *Drosophila* to bacteria, and bacteriophage, a virus that lives on bacteria; people referred to it as "phage." The researchers who moved to center stage now had been trained as biochemists, microbiologists, and most often, physicists. Their interest was in the concrete, physical nature of the gene—its molecular structure.

"With the new men came new programs," according to one historian of science. He was speaking of a small community known as the phage group, the most conspicuous of the new men. "With their fastidious rigor, their insistence on the simplest biological systems ... their self-conscious marking off of the group from others—their snobbery—the phage group has attracted attention even to a disproportionate degree."

Max Delbrück, the elder statesman of the phage group, was a physicist, educated at Göttingen, Germany. Later he went to Denmark to study with Niels Bohr, who had won the Nobel prize in physics for his work on atomic structure. He then went to CalTech, where he joined ongoing work with phage.

In 1944, the same year McClintock was elected President of the Genetics Society, researchers at the Rockefeller Institute published the first proof that genes are made of the substance DNA, deoxyribonucleic acid. This chemical holds the instructions for all the workings of the cells—all the chemicals that will be made by the cell, and all the cellular reactions caused by the chemicals. By passing on hereditary information from one generation of cells to the next it serves as a set of master blueprints.

Nobody knew how DNA worked its magic, nobody knew its structure, and, in fact, some eight years were to pass before the scientific community accepted this discovery. Meanwhile Max Delbrück began a series of summer courses in phage at Cold Spring Harbor. This was a crash program for researchers trained in the physical sciences and it attracted people with established reputations who were eager to explore the new frontier.

One graduate student who came to study with Delbrück was James Watson. He took the phage course in 1948 when he was 20. The tall, thin, twitchily nervous young man was determined to become famous while still young enough to enjoy it. Openly scornful of women scientists, Watson's later account of his first summer at Cold Spring Harbor made only one mention of Barbara McClintock's presence there, and it had to do with playing baseball next to her cornfield, "into which the ball too often went."

After earning his Ph.D. Watson went abroad for postdoctoral studies, eventually making his way to Cambridge University. There, with Francis Crick, he uncovered the structure of DNA in 1953. He described it as a double helix—a double thread held together by crosspieces, and coiled like a spring. In other words, it resembled a twisted rope ladder.

Before a cell divides, the DNA splits down the middle and forms two strands, each consisting of one sidepiece of the ladder and its attached rungs. Each strand then builds a new opposite half by linking up with spare parts present in the cell nucleus. The cell now contains two DNA ladders identical to the original.

Within the scientific community and beyond it, the Watson-Crick double helix was hailed as a major, and brilliant, discovery. Yet many important problems remained.

How do the genes contribute to behavior? How does the egg develop into the organism, with all its vast diversity, when the DNA replicated in all these cells was identical to the DNA in the first cell? Was change in the genetic material a gradual process—one solely due to random mutation and natural selection, as the naturalist Charles Darwin had proposed?

But supreme self-confidence was a characteristic of the phage group; they believed they would find the answers as surely as they had found the structure of DNA, by attacking the smallest and simplest form of life. Certainly they never expected answers from classical geneticists, such as those working with maize, an experimental material that was cumbersome, intricate, and took half a year to mature. Bacteria and phage, which could reproduce in a matter of minutes, seemed more promising.

———

For some years McClintock had been studying mutation in corn plants, and the repeated rounds of chromosome breakage and fusion that caused them. Of particular interest to her were maize kernels with spots, or dots; it had long been suspected that these multi-colored kernels were the result of mutation that took place during the development of the corn.

In the winter of 1944 McClintock saw a pattern of pigmentation on a few kernels that was unlike anything she had come across before. The spots were not random, but distributed in a way that suggested a kind of genetic instability under some form of regulation. And each kernel showed its own characteristic frequency of mutation, which could be seen in the size and number of its spots. Furthermore, there were patches of corn-husk tissue that showed a rate of mutation different from that of the plant as a whole.

McClintock suspected that something, some event, must have taken place in the course of the plant's development to alter its genetic properties. For two years she pursued this event. "It never occurred to me" she said later, "that there was going to be any stumbling block. Not that I had the answer, but [I had] the joy of going at it. When you have that joy, you do the right experiments. You let the material tell you where to go, and it tells you at every step."

After two years she had begun to see a pattern of genetic elements that acted as switches—"controlling elements," she called them. Moreover, these controlling elements moved. The time and frequency of their movements seemed to be connected to the developmental cycle of the plant and kernel, as if they responded to signals from the plant as a whole. McClintock called this mechanism "transposition," and reported it in a paper sent to the Carnegie Yearbook.

Nobody—no scientist at any rate—read the yearbook, a fact of which she was well aware, just as she was aware that mainstream scientists of the late 1940s considered gene material to be fixed in place. There was essentially nobody at Cold Spring Harbor with whom she could discuss this work that contradicted every accepted belief. She wrote regularly to Marcus Rhoades, who was sympathetic and kind, yet she doubted he understood. She continued filing her yearly reports, but was almost entirely alone now, withdrawn from the scientific community, indeed withdrawn from others in general.

By 1951 McClintock had overwhelming evidence that the genes that determine such characteristics as color were manipulated by genetic controlling elements, whose locations on the chromosomes were unfixed. One controlling element—she called it the "dissociator"—was responsible for suppressing the activity of the pigment gene. Another, the "activator," controlled the dissociator, commanding it to jump into action alongside a particular structural gene. Every part of her theory was scientific heresy.

The evidence supporting these heresies filled several filing cabinets and a 95-page unpublished manuscript, meticulously researched, closely reasoned, elegant in structure. It was the result of six years' work, all of it done with tools that seemed to belong to the nineteenth century. Her scientific peers, the molecular biologists, used sophisticated new techniques—radioisotopes, atomic-level x-ray crystallography, and the electron microscope, capable of seeing molecules. McClintock used only the ordinary microscope, cross-breeding, and observation. But it was the observation of a scientist to whom each ear of corn was an individual, a member of her family, and the brilliantly colored kernels were as carefully observed as the traits of a growing child.

She planned to present a paper explaining her work at the next Cold Spring Harbor Symposium, in 1951.

The writing of a scientific paper is not the cut-and-dried task it might seem, not a simple setting forth of evidence, followed by a statement of what that evidence proves. It must persuade. It must take its audience by the hand and lead it step by step through that mounting pile of evidence, never for a moment losing the audience's attention, till the conclusion is reached and seems inevitable.

When the evidence is extremely intricate and the conclusion unusual—wildly unusual, as hers was—the quality of persuasion must match the challenge.

McClintock had never enjoyed writing, and knew her style was hard to follow. A colleague at Missouri remembers her bringing a paper to one of the department members, a man who wrote easily and well. She asked if he had any suggestions to improve her writing, and with a few quick strokes he rewrote one paragraph, making it vivid, immediate, "till it leaped from the page." But she shook her head. She had to admit it worked, she said, but it didn't sound at all like her.

She wrote in the passive voice, which most scientific journals require, but hers seemed almost excessively passive, and without vividness or immediacy. It was easy to become bored when reading or listening to McClintock, not because the material was in itself boring, but because of the style, the complexity of her reasoning, and the many items that had to be kept in mind for a full understanding of the whole.

Moreover, she was a mystic by nature, who tended to think intuitively. Stephen Jay Gould, a Harvard naturalist and widely published writer, calls it "a kind of global, intuitive insight," utterly different from the logical thinking to which experimental scientists are accustomed. In 1951 her audience would include many former physicists and biochemists, most of them relentlessly logical.

That summer's symposium at Cold Spring Harbor attracted about 100 participants from all over the world. Most of the eminent figures in genetics were among them. McClintock delivered her paper on the morning of the first day to an audience that listened in silence.

When she finished there were no questions. She thought she heard actual complaints, even heard some people snickering. It "really knocked" her, she said later. "It

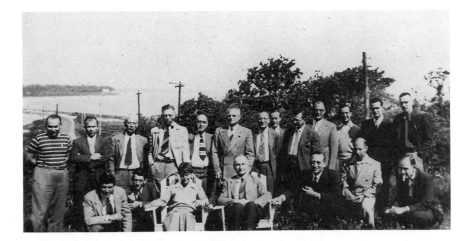

June 1949. Barbara McClintock is the sole woman at a meeting of scientists. She was working in the genetics department at the Cold Spring Harbor facility at the time.

was just a surprise that I couldn't communicate; it was a surprise that I was being ridiculed, or being told that I was really mad."

According to Allan Campbell, a graduate student at the time, now a Stanford biologist, "What they did not appreciate was the significance of her findings. . . . The time was not ripe." Her ideas were too new, there were no accepted terms for her concepts. More important still, her paper was overshadowed by current work on phage—the technological triumphs of the molecular biologists.

She tried again during the next five years in seminars both at Cold Spring Harbor and elsewhere, each time with the same response—silence, broken by mumbling and shoulder-shrugging. She stopped giving talks. Although she never stopped working, she published only in the annual reports that no one read. She lived in two rooms over a garage, took long walks in the woods, and pursued her studies of Tibetan Buddhism. A small circle of friends continued to cherish and protect her, and the Carnegie administrators "never said anything to me that was discouraging. They certainly must have known what my other colleagues were saying about me, but they did not let it come to me."

She no longer minded being ignored.... She'd adjusted to it, adjusted to the belief that she was "absolutely crazy"—or, in the words of one famous geneticist, "Just an old broad who's been hanging around Cold Spring Harbor for years."

In 1960 McClintock came across a paper published in a French journal, proposing a system called the "operon," composed of a structural gene and a regulator gene. This system closely resembled her own controlling elements. Greatly excited, she called a staff seminar at Cold Spring Harbor, wrote a paper for *American Naturalist,* and sent a copy to the authors of the French work.

Their names were François Jacob and Jacques Monod, specialists in a bacterium called *E. coli,* and she had known Monod for years, "since he was a little boy in science." They met for the first time in 1936 at CalTech, when Monod was in his mid-20s, a slender young man, as charming and handsome as he was reckless. Returning to France in 1938, he married, and started work for a doctorate. Then war broke out. France fell to the Germans, and Monod joined the Resistance. By 1944 he was chief of military operations for an umbrella organization combining all Resistance forces—on the run, never sleeping twice in the same place. Captured by the Gestapo, escaping from the Gestapo, he somehow managed to continue research at the Pasteur Institute.

Now he had come to McClintock's rescue, or so it

seemed. In their longer paper for an American journal, Monod and Jacob failed to mention McClintock's work—an unhappy oversight, Monod later admitted. But in the summer of 1961 he tried to make up for the oversight. Summarizing the Cold Spring Harbor Symposium, he said: "Long before regulator genes and operator were recognized in bacteria, the extensive and penetrating work of McClintock ... had revealed the existence, in maize, of two classes of genetic 'controlling elements'. . . ."

Nevertheless, that summer's excitement was trained exclusively on the work of the two French scientists. McClintock had thought—she'd been convinced—that once people saw the confirmation of her controlling elements, she would then have their full attention for the rest of her vision— transposition, the genetic material that jumped, and that people referred to as "jumping genes," to show how laughable they were.

But this failed to happen. Even Monod and Jacob had little to say about the movable elements; they had the mindset of molecular biologists, members of what Monod called "the phage church," and they didn't understand maize, were unable to see why maize mattered.

Although McClintock insisted she was not discouraged, she vowed that never again would she give a seminar at Cold Spring Harbor.

In 1968, six years after he was awarded the Nobel Prize for his revolutionary work with DNA, James Watson became director of the Cold Spring Harbor Laboratories. Barbara McClintock was still there, still living in two rooms over a green-painted garage, still working hard at the age of sixty-six. When people at Cold Spring Harbor thought of her at all it was as a relic of earlier times, a little woman who had

Dr. McClintock poses for photographers the day her Nobel Prize was announced.

once been important for research into something or other, but was now a mystic of some sort. "Absolutely off-the-wall," according to one fellow-scientist.

Change, when it came, started at the high-tech forefront. Aided by the powerful new tools of genetic engineering, experiments in the 1970s showed that bits of the DNA did indeed jump around, on and between three DNA elements found in bacteria. Were there mobile genetic elements in higher organisms as well?

In time it became apparent that this was true for every organism examined—yeast, worms, fruit flies—and that the implications were enormous. The jumping genes are expected to provide insights into a number of major mysteries: how whole organisms develop from single cells; how entirely new species arise; why some cells occasionally go berserk, as happens in cancer; how white blood cells can make antibodies so quickly in response to infection.

In the words of James Watson, McClintock "is a very remarkable person, fiercely independent, beholden to no one. Her work is of fundamental importance."

Suddenly everyone was talking about McClintock. Geneticists "embraced her pioneering discoveries as though they were long-lost relations," according to *Newsweek*. Honors and prizes thrust her into the spotlight. In the year 1981 she won the Albert Lasker Basic Medical Research Award of $15,000; Israel's Wolf Foundation Prize of $50,000; and a tax-free annual fellowship for life of $60,000 from the MacArthur Foundation. She bought a new car and moved out of the two rooms into more spacious quarters. But for a person who had little use for money, and none whatever for fame, it was too much at once. *Newsweek* remarked: "Seated primly before a roomful of reporters, Barbara McClintock was plainly miserable."

Two years later she won the Nobel Prize, the first woman to win it alone for medicine. Because she had no telephone the news came to her by radio. Afterward she put on jeans and heavy shoes and went for her usual walk through the woods, gathering walnuts along the way.

Today, at eighty-seven, Barbara McClintock's habits have hardly changed. She works every day, either in the cornfield or in her laboratory, and always alone. She shrinks from publicity of any kind, is made genuinely uncomfortable by it, and her work continues to bring her joy.

In her words, "I can't imagine a better life."

CHAPTER 4

Rita Levi-Montalcini

RITA LEVI-MONTALCINI:

1986 Nobel Prize for Medicine

"THE HALO OF NERVE FIBERS"

A friend had come to visit, someone Rita Levi-Montalcini had known at medical school a few years earlier. When he asked how her work was coming along, and what she was doing these days, she was unable to answer. What could she possibly be doing? What was left for her to do? The Jews of Italy were forbidden to practice the professions; therefore, she could no longer work as a doctor. As for her medical research, that, too, had come to an end. The University of Turin, like other institutions of learning throughout the country, was closed to Jews. It was against the law for her to attend lectures, to use the laboratories, or even the library.

But the doctor's silence seemed to irritate the visitor. "One doesn't lose heart in the face of the first difficulties," he told her. Why not set up a small laboratory at home, and take up her interrupted research there?

She thought it over, turning it this way and that way inside her mind, already excited by the possibility. It would be a voyage of adventure to unknown lands, carried out in defiance of the racial laws, secretly, in her own small bedroom. She even knew what piece of work she wanted to do, because of a paper she'd read one summer day while riding in the open wagon of a livestock train the year before.

With a beloved friend beside her, she had been sitting on the floor of the wagon, her legs dangling over the side as they made their way toward a mountain village. The friend was whistling; his hand gripped her arm to keep her from slipping out of the wagon. The doctor read the research paper while breathing in sweet summer air and the smell of freshly cut hay. And the paper had to do with the growth of nerve fibers in chick embryos—an exploration into the "jungle" of the nervous system, it seemed to her at the time. It was written by an American, unknown to her, by the name of Viktor Hamburger. She had longed to learn more, to test the author's conclusions for herself. Now she saw it as the perfect experiment to be carried out at home, in a makeshift laboratory in the bedroom.

But first it would be necessary to get permission from the rest of the family. Her mother agreed immediately; anything was better than another separation, such as the one before the outbreak of war, when Rita went to work in Belgium for a time. As for Paola, Rita's twin sister, she was an artist, whose work had been unaffected by the racial laws. She wanted Rita to have the same chance. Gino, their older brother, was ready to help in any way he could. Although an architect by profession, he'd been trained as an engineer, and he promised to hunt up and help install equipment. They would need incubators, microscopes, some surgical tools.

That was how everything began, early in 1941, three years after the racial laws were put in place, two years after the start of World War II. The doctor was now a little past thirty and hungry for the new adventure.

Rita Levi-Montalcini was born in 1909, in the city of Turin in northern Italy. It has been described as a melancholy place, smelling of soot and industry, with heavy mists rising from the Po river. Turin is gray, busy, serious-minded. High mountains surround it. Switzerland is only a bicycle ride away.

The twins, Rita and Paola, were the youngest of four children. Their mother, Adele Montalcini, was "a marvelous woman—intelligent, sensitive, artistic," according to Rita, and very beautiful, a tall blonde with a serious, thoughtful expression. In Rita's eyes she had only one flaw: she was by nature submissive. She never seemed to mind that her husband decided everything.

Adamo Levi, their father, an electrical engineer with a talent for mathematics, had built a factory on the outskirts of Turin for ice-making and the distilling of alcohol. Broad-shouldered, with piercing dark eyes and a great curving mustache, he was subject to brief but violent outbursts of temper; his sisters, who loved him, called him "Damino the Terrible," and from her earliest childhood Rita had been afraid of him. "A wonderful human being," she recalled, "exceedingly nice to me, and very gentle, but . . ."

When she was little, and the time came to kiss him goodnight, she would turn her head away from his face, sending the kiss into the air. He sometimes remarked, with sadness, "Rita . . . would rather kiss the air than her father." He kept trying to overcome the barrier between them—they both did, but there it was, one of the mysteries of personality. None of the other children were afraid of him, not Gino, not their older sister Anna, and certainly not Paola, who adored him.

The twins, Rita and Paola, were tied together by such powerful bonds of affection that Rita thought of Paola as being part of herself. Paola was the shorter of the two, blue-eyed, with features like her father's, while Rita resembled her mother's mother; her gray-green eyes held a melancholy expression. She was anxious, timid, without self-confidence. The entire adult world was frightening to her, as well as "monsters that might suddenly pop out of the dark and throw themselves upon me." But mostly it was her father, his temper, the quick flaring of his nostrils before he lost his temper, and his "imperious" ways. She had nothing to do with other children in those days; she chose either to be alone or with her other self, Paola.

"I had a feeling I was not bright enough," she recalled in later years. "I was very stupid as a child." All the same she came to believe that somewhere inside her was a core of strength inherited from her father. He was the one, she said, who taught her to admire energy, ingenuity, and serious dedication to work. He was the one who gave shape to her life, yet somehow she only realized it after he died.

If Rita's childhood was lonely, she was always aware of belonging to a large, affectionate family of people who valued culture and intellect. Besides the family at home, there were aunts, uncles, and many cousins. Some were observant Jews; others had intermarried with Catholics; still others, like the Levi-Montalcinis, took no interest in religion. Beyond this extended family was yet another, the community of Turin Jews, only a few thousand, mostly prosperous, well-educated, liberal in their politics, and deeply devoted to Italy. Many had been there for centuries—the Montalcinis, the family of Rita's mother, traced their ancestry to two centuries before Christ.

There was lingering anti-Semitism in Italy, but it was hidden, subterranean, and nobody took it seriously. When children in the park asked Rita what religion her family belonged to, her father told her to say, "I am a freethinker." He assured her that when she was twenty-one she could choose to be a Jew, a Catholic, or to go on as before; meanwhile, she was not to worry about religion.

The little girls were in elementary school when Italy entered the first World War on the side of the Allied powers—Britain, France, then America. Rita hoped this war would go on long enough for her to become a Red Cross nurse at the front. To be a doctor was clearly impossible—she had never seen a woman doctor.

During that same period a young journalist with the name of Benito Amilcare Andrea Mussolini, a blacksmith's son, was called to active duty in the trenches. A fervent Socialist, he believed in abolishing private property; all people were to be equal, none richer or more powerful than another. Yet seven years later, in 1921, as the head of the Fascist party, he became Il Duce, the absolute ruler of Italy.

When the twins were done with elementary school, a middle school had to be chosen. This was an important decision, because some middle schools led to those high schools that in turn led to university. Others did not; these other high schools had no classes in mathematics, Latin, or Greek, all necessary for university. They led to technical institutes or teachers' training or to the destiny for which most young women were headed, marriage and motherhood.

The decision would naturally be made by their father. And even though all three daughters had shown themselves to be superior students, he saw no point to a university career. His two sisters, he said, went on to university, and their marriages suffered from it. His little girls were not to suffer. They were to become happy wives and mothers. They would devote themselves to their families, to the management of large households with the help of several servants. They would give parties—"receptions"—and wear lovely clothes, and leave all troublesome matters in the hands of their husbands.

The decision was, of course, final. Anna, the eldest, married early and forgot her desire to become a writer. Paola already knew she intended to be an artist, for which university training was unnecessary. And Rita had no idea what she was meant to be. She felt she was without talents, without interests. She attended the middle school that did not lead to college, went on to the high school for girls, and "drifted along in the dark," trying to fill the emptiness of her days by reading. She made few friends; other girls talked only about boys and dresses, which bored her.

The twins were seventeen when they finished high school. By then Paola had found a place in the workshop of a well-known painter, and Rita was still aimless, still without hope. She was almost twenty before a tragic occurrence showed the way out of the blind alley she'd wandered into.

A family servant by the name of Giovanna was found to have stomach cancer. Giovanna had been with the twins from the time they were born, a second mother, one of the fixed stars of their childhood. On the day Giovanna went into hospital for surgery, Rita vowed to herself that she would take up her studies again and go into medicine.

Giovanna died with Rita holding her hand and Mother and Paola standing by the bedside. Her death was a loss for all of them, but to Rita it only affirmed the vow she had taken.

When she told her mother about it, Mother encouraged her to speak to Father. She would have to explain that she had no desire to marry, no vocation for marriage or children. "In my family I saw that I could not ever accomplish anything, to be married, like my mother was." How was she to face her father and say these words?

She finally found the courage to go to him and tell him what she wanted to do. He listened intently. He reminded her that the course of study was long, difficult, unsuited for a woman. Besides, she would have several subjects to make up.

Rita told him she would study privately with the help of a tutor. With the greatest reluctance he gave his permission. During the next eight months she threw herself "headlong into this program which had become the very reason of my existence." Photographs from that time show her as very thin, her dark hair cut short and drawn severely back; her eyes are large and sad, with a level, head-on look that seems to be characteristic of her.

In 1918 Benito Mussolini, the journalist, had returned from combat to a country exhausted by its war effort. Raw materials were depleted, the merchant fleet shattered. Thousands could find no work and the government was bankrupt.

There was more. When postwar treaties were made at Versailles, the Allied powers all but ignored their promises to Italy—they got little in the way of territory, and Italian pride was crushed. It began to seem that their many thousands of war dead had sacrificed themselves for nothing.

Riots followed street-fighting; there was an endless cycle of labor strikes. Many turned to Communism, a revolutionary brand of Socialism that had overthrown Russia's tsarist regime in 1917. Mussolini, the former Socialist, now made a complete about-face. Early in 1919 he put together what was to become the Fascist party, declaring war on both Communism and Socialism. At the time his party numbered about 150, but within the next three years it grew from a loose-knit collection of gangs—thugs and street bullies— into a military organization. In 1922 they threatened to march on Rome and destroy it, unless King Victor Emmanuel appointed Mussolini his prime minister.

The king remembered how the Russian tsar was shot to death by revolutionaries, and gave in. By 1925 constitutional government had come to an end; opposition parties were disbanded, the free press outlawed, and Mussolini ruled as dictator. He was now thirty-nine years old, short, broad, with a massive jutting jaw, hypnotic eyes, and clean-shaven head. He was said to love little children. Perhaps he loved Italy. Certainly Mussolini loved power—uniforms, weapons, cheering crowds who cried out his name. He dreamed of building an empire.

In 1930 Rita Levi-Montalcini passed the university entrace exams at the head of the list of those who had studied at home; she started medical school in the autumn.

A friend of hers recalls the dark, smoky halls where classes were held—cavernous halls full of dust, century-old ghosts, and rows of glass-doored cupboards packed with slips of paper that mice had gnawed at. On crowded benches in the semicircular classroom, freshmen and sophomores together took the two-year course in human anatomy. There were some 300 young men, seven women, and, in the middle of the room, a cadaver. According to Levi-

Montalcini, the lectures were "tremendously boring," but at the end of the first year she passed her exams with honors.

Years later a fellow student told her, "in those days you were just impossible, a kind of squid ready to squirt ink at anybody who came near you." But she made a few friends, some of them friends she was to value forever. And there was one student, Guido Boni, who left a deep mark on her life.

She describes him as "extremely tall, with a penetrating gaze, musketeer mustache and a curious way of walking, head down and always whistling a Beethoven symphony or an aria of Schubert's or Mozart's." Guido was the whistler who sat beside her that day in the wagon, when she first read the research paper about chick embryos.

Together they went for evening strolls in Valentino Park near the university, or rode off to the countryside on his motorcycle. "When I listen, more than half a century after, to Schubert's C Major Quintet . . . I relive those hours spent in the park or on outings when I . . . tried not to fall off the pillion of the motorcycle he drove skillfully but fast up the steep stony tracks of the valley." This closeness was to endure throughout the years that followed graduation and the war.

With the first year of medical school behind her, Levi-Montalcini decided to become an intern at the Institute of Anatomy, in order to study under an extraordinary man named Giuseppe Levi. A celebrated scientist and known anti-Fascist, Levi was not related to her, but he so resembled her father that he might have been Adamo Levi's brother or double.

Giuseppe Levi had a daughter, Natalia, who became a friend of Rita's. Natalia recalls ". . . the nightmare of our father's outbursts of fury which exploded unexpectedly and often for the pettiest reason: a pair of shoes that could not be found, a book out of its proper place. . . ." He had thick red hair, bushy eyebrows, and walked clumsily, barrelling forward with his head bent down, and his voice was loud; it was loud even when he believed he was whispering. "His anger filled me with terror," Levi-Montalcini remembers, but all the same she and five others—two of whom were to become, like her, Nobel laureates—chose to spend their second year as the apprentices of this noisy, temperamental, brilliant man.

They began with histology, the microscopic examination of plant and animal tissue. These tissues, sliced paper-thin and stained with silver solution, were arranged on glass slides and put under primitive microscopes that might have been left over from the seventeenth century. None of the six students was in any way interested in histology.

Later that year Levi-Montalcini was set to work counting nerve cells in the spinal ganglia, those little clumps to the left and right of the spinal vertebrae. Later still she was to study the formation of tissues, especially nerve tissues, "in vitro," meaning in a glass dish. It was a topic that Guiseppe Levi had worked on for some years, with passionate enthusiasm. Soon this passion infected Levi-Montalcini. She began to see Professor Levi in a different light. There developed between them what she calls "a Master-disciple relationship, characterized by ever-increasing affection and esteem."

But the years at the university were marred by an unexpected and grievous loss. In 1932 her father began suffering from chest pains. Early one summer morning he died of heart failure, lying in bed under a painting his wife had made for him just before their wedding. "I kissed his forehead," Rita remembers, "and thought with anguish of the kisses I had been unable to give him in my childhood."

Levi-Montalcini was graduated from medical school with top honors in 1936, and began a three-year postgraduate course in neurology and psychiatry. At the university's neurology clinic she saw patients, poor people unable to afford private doctors. There were times when she thought she wanted to leave research and devote herself solely to the practice of medicine, but at other times she wanted both.

The year 1938 put an end to this inner debate. Mussolini had decided to ally himself with Adolf Hitler, the Nazi dictator who had come to power in Germany five years earlier. Italian Fascism and German Nazism had many similarities, but there were differences as well. For one thing, Hitler wanted to rid the world of Jews, to make it *Judenrein,* meaning "Jew-clean." His hatred of Jews amounted to a mania. Mussolini, on the other hand, had nothing against the Jews—one of his many mistresses had been Jewish. But to win Hitler's approval, he was ready to sacrifice the Jews of Italy.

An anti-Semitic campaign began, at first slowly, unofficially. Then in the autumn of 1938 the racial laws were declared. Jews were now forbidden to marry non-Jews, to work in the professions, to teach, to belong to state firms or institutions.

Italians were not quick to take up this legal anti-Semitism. Supreme individualists, they never much cared for taking orders. Besides, it was by no means clear to them who was Jewish and who was not. Italians, dark-haired and dark-eyed, look much like Jews.

A Jewish friend of Rita's recalled that when he was at the university no one directed to him a single hostile word or gesture. Yet he imagined that "I could feel them withdraw . . . a minuscule but perceptible flash of mistrust or suspicion," so that he wondered what they thought of him, whether he was the same to them as he had been six months ago, or had perhaps become the Jew, who, "as Dante put it, 'In your midst, laughs at you.' "

Yet nothing was said. In the laboratories, life seemed to go on as it always had. Levi-Montalcini felt uncomfortable all the same, and in March of 1939 she accepted an invitation from an institute in Brussels, Belgium. Giuseppe Levi was nearby, in Liège, and she went to visit his laboratory on weekends. They talked about many things, but tried not to talk about Hitler and Germany, and the smell of war that pervaded the continent.

In September of that year Hitler invaded Poland; Great Britain and France immediately declared that a state of war existed. By Christmas Eve Levi-Montalcini was once again home in Turin with her family. She was unable to work, even to study, but at least they were together.

Hitler's armies captured Paris, and France surrendered to him. Southern Italy came under intensive bombing by the British. Giuseppe Levi's son-in-law, the husband of his daughter, Natalia, was arrested, not as a Jew but as a known anti-Fascist. And throughout the country, thousands of foreign-born Jews—mostly refugees from Hitler—were rounded up and herded into internment camps. Who could tell what would become of them?

But there was the laboratory in the bedroom—a challenge, a distraction, ultimately a refuge. All during the winter of 1940 and the spring that followed, Gino and Rita assembled its component parts, burying themselves in the problem of creating precision instruments out of whatever they could find. Ordinary sewing needles, sharpened on a fine grindstone, were transformed into surgical tools. Two small thermostats became incubators. Rita managed to buy a stereomicroscope and a binocular Zeiss microscope, both horribly expensive. There was miscellaneous glassware, and a glass box, heat-regulated, with two openings in front that Gino designed so his sister could insert her arms and operate on her embryos under the microscope without fear of infection.

By summer's end everything was miraculously fitted in. Then Giuseppe Levi came back from Belgium, haggard and pale after a dangerous trip across Germany. When Rita asked him if he cared to join in the new research he agreed with pleasure, thus becoming, to her great pride, her first and only assistant. The experiments began.

It was a time when little was known about the development of the nervous system. By the mid-nineteenth century the human body was seen to consists of cells, but only at the turn of the century was it agreed that the nervous system too consisted of cells—until then people preferred to believe that the brain, the human brain, where the soul lived, was sacred and exempt from physical laws.

The next step would be learning how these nerve cells grew and developed. Beyond this question was another more important, more baffling question, one still unanswered today: how does a single fertilized cell, from which the embryo grows, turn into the complex organism made up of many billions of cells with different forms and functions—brain, liver, eyes.

Researchers at that time were using chick embryos because they developed quickly, and broadly speaking the physiology was the same in all vertebrates. The American whose paper Rita had read tried to find out what happened when the beginning limbs of chick embryos were nipped off. What became of the beginning nerve cells that were supposed to migrate toward those limbs and form its network of nerve fibers?

He saw that a week after the operation, the nerve cells in question dwindled and died. When an extra limb was grafted on, nerve cells flourished. So there must be some kind of organizing substance in the cutoff limb—an "inductive factor," he called it—in whose absence the nerve cells died out.

Snipping off limb buds, examining nerve cells, the two researchers in the makeshift laboratory repeated this experiment day after day, while Hitler's armies invaded Europe and marched triumphantly toward Russia. The civilized world was falling apart, but the researchers huddled over their microscope and scribbled their notes. They did it, Rita said later, because at certain times you will do anything to keep from facing a reality that might drive you to self-destruction. She never for a moment thought of it as important work—work that would further her career or push forward the frontiers of science. It was what she could do at the time, what she enjoyed doing, and what she had to do to keep her sanity.

And she did it with enormous patience, aided by the gift of sharp eyes and rock-steady hands. She took samples from her embryos when they were three days old, and at brief intervals—almost hour by hour—from then on to the end of a twenty-day incubation period. This was done over and over and over, with different specimens.

That summer Allied air forces began bombing the cities of northern Italy, especially Turin, because of its many factories. The bombs came at night when the planes were safe from antiaircraft batteries—almost every night, it seemed. First the whine of the air-raid siren, then the rush to the basement, although the family knew they were in danger of being buried alive there amid the ruins of a bombed-out building. Rita always brought her Zeiss microscope to the basement. "It was very precious to me," she said, "I couldn't live without it."

So fear was their daily diet, fear not only of the bombs, but the fear they had carried with them from the start of the war—that the Allies might not win, that Europe would be conquered by the German-Italian partners. Only their mother seemed untroubled. She was sure they would all die, but had somehow convinced herself that they would die together, and this gave her great courage.

When daylight came and the bombings stopped, Rita returned with her microscope to the laboratory that was her private island. She had begun to see the development of "nerve centers" and circuits in a different light—not fixed, rigid, as the textbooks showed, but changing and dynamic. There was something—a mysterious substance—that kept the cell metabolism in motion, allowing the cell to use material in its environment for growth and survival. This substance existed in the outer parts of the embryo, and signaled to oncoming nerve fibers, reaching out to them, luring them on toward their destination. It was what scientists call a "trophic factor," and when it failed to meet the nerve fibers as they approached the cutoff limb, they gave up their journey. But there must have been some of it in the tissues in between or they would never have started that journey.

"Only by following from hour to hour, as in a cinematographic sequence, the development of nerve centers and circuits, did I come to realize how dynamic these processes are; how individual cells behave in a way similar to that of living beings," Rita later explained. There was no "inductive factor," no organizer. There was only change, adaptation, and the mysterious substance about which she knew nothing so far except that it existed.

Allied bombing intensified that autumn, and the family moved to the countryside. In a little cottage, about an hour away from Turin, Rita set up her laboratory on the dining table; when the needed parts had been plucked from the egg yolks with watchmakers' forceps, she took the rest to the kitchen and made omelettes. By day she traveled by train to Turin to meet Giuseppe Levi and write up their results, which were sent to a Belgian journal for publication.

The following summer Italy surrendered to Allied forces, and German troops massed at its northern borders, ready to invade the country that was formerly its partner. Until then, not a single Jew, whether foreign or native-born, had been handed over to the Nazis by Italian police, but now the SS, an especially ruthless branch of the Nazi military, was on its way. Italians knew little about extermination camps where Jews were burned or gassed to death, nor did they know the SS had quotas to fill. Each week a certain number of Jews were to be sent to Auschwitz and other places with unfamiliar names. But they knew they had to leave the north and find hiding places out of reach of the Germans, perhaps in the territories already occupied by invading British and American forces.

"As far as my family was concerned . . . we knew that a delay of days, perhaps even of hours, might cost us our lives," Rita said later. They were back in Turin at the time, having thought that Italy's surrender meant they were out of danger, and they knew that local Fascists had been asking their neighbors the whereabouts of Adamo Levi's family. The neighbors pretended they'd never heard of Adamo Levi, but there were German tanks outside the central railway station now. The German military was directing city traffic. And Eichmann, the man Hitler put in charge of exterminating the Jews, had sent teams of experienced Jew-hunters.

They talked about fleeing to Switzerland. At the last minute Anna's family did succeed in making it to Switzerland, but Rita, Paola, their mother, Gino, and the young wife he had married between air raids, simply got on a train and headed south, having no plan, no idea where they were going.

Impulsively they got off at Florence and went to the home of a friend of a friend; they carried false identity papers, clumsily made, and gave false names, and prayed their landlady would not see through the deception. She told them they were welcome to stay so long as they were not Jews. She had many Jewish friends, she said, but could not afford to endanger her father, who was old and very sick. They assured her they were Catholics from Apulia in the south and that their home had been destroyed by Allied bombs.

Afterward they came to realize that the landlady knew all along, and would never have betrayed them. Throughout Italy, Jews were in hiding in churches, convents, as well as private homes, sheltered by non-Jews at great personal danger. There were of course betrayals, although very few. And some people were killed because they never believed themselves to be in danger; Jews in Rome, who had simply waited at home, were rounded up by German occupation forces, crammed into cattle cars, and shipped off to the gas chambers and ovens to fill quotas.

In Florence, Guido Boni came to visit, sometimes alone,

sometimes with one or two friends, all using false names. They belonged to Partito di Azione, one of the groups of partisans fighting the Germans as guerrillas from hidden headquarters in the mountains or forests. Guido came to keep Rita informed about the resistance movement, as well as for personal reasons. She longed to join him, but knew she never would, not only because she could not abandon her mother, but also, as Guido put it, because she was not cut out for being a conspirator—she lacked presence of mind, he said, and would have endangered her comrades if captured.

Guido wanted them to marry. "We were engaged," she recalls. "He loved me very much, and we were for many years together . . ." but she had resolved never to marry, never to live with another person, and have to adjust her life to that other person. . . . Meanwhile, she and Paola forged identity papers for the partisans, papers that would fool no one except Italians, who were willing to be fooled.

The following summer—1944—the Nazis mined and destroyed several of the bridges of Florence, and the city was virtually cut off, without food, electricity, or water. There was fighting between German and partisan forces, various parts of the city falling to one side or the other. The war was everywhere; it seemed to Rita that the battlefront ran right down the street where they lived. But people went out on the streets all the same, great crowds of them carrying their most precious possessions, fleeing the Germans, hoping for the momentary arrival of Allied armies.

On the second of November, as British forces marched silently through the streets of Florence, she saw a bus marked with the Jewish Star of David, distributing water. There was no more need for false names and false identity papers. Hungry, thirsty, exhausted by the long ordeal, Jews became themselves again.

Of 45,000 Jews in Italy at the start of the German occupation, all but 6,800 survived to see the day of liberation.

Sporadic fighting continued, but the war was essentially over. Levi-Montalcini went to the Allies' health services to volunteer as a doctor. She was immediately set to work in an old military barracks where refugees were cared for, becoming both doctor and nurse. Trucks arrived each night, unloaded their charges in the barracks yard, and she had to check their condition, then see them settled somewhere within the shed—old people and children suffering from malnutrition, newborn babies painfully dehydrated. She suffered along with them, "an impotent witness to the extinguishing of the lives of these small creatures, by then already on the threshhold of death."

An outbreak of typhoid fever became epidemic, the death toll climbing to fifty a day. Now she worked with the knowledge that she herself might die along with her patients. But by risking her life for them she was almost able to forget her sense of guilt for not having joined the partisans.

In this military barracks soldiers came and went, including many Americans, all young, healthy, well fed. It seemed to her they looked down on the Italians when they troubled to look at them at all—a defeated people, starved, ragged, foreign. An enemy people, formerly led by the Fascist Mussolini. She would have liked to explain that Mussolini was not her leader or her family's. But why bother? They were so young, these soldiers. Drunk with victory and Italian wine, they would never have listened to her.

In April of 1945, just before the Allied armies reached Milan, she heard that Mussolini was caught by Italian partisans as he tried to make his way to Switzerland, disguised as a German officer. The partisans executed him on the spot, along with his young mistress.

One month later Rita went home to Turin. Everywhere in Italy people were going home. Giuseppe Levi's daughter, Natalia, returned to Turin with three little fatherless children. Her husband, Leone Ginzburg, had died in a Roman prison named Regina Coeli, Queen of Heaven, where many Jews and partisans died. Natalia said later, "We shall not get over this war. It's useless to try.... Something has happened to our houses. Something has happened to us. We shall never be at peace again. We have seen reality's darkest face and it no longer horrifies us.... We are a people without tears."

The partisans left their hiding places in the forests and mountains and made their way to their homes, Guido Boni among them; in time he resumed his medical practice. Rita's older sister, Anna, came back safely from Switzerland with her family. Paola, Mother, Gino and his wife returned some months later, all feeling like convalescents after a long illness, numbed, without appetite.

Rita no longer cared about the secret laboratory where once she had lived like Robinson Crusoe. Nor did she care to continue in medicine. She had suffered too much from the deaths of her patients in the barracks; a doctor needed to be more objective. She enrolled in biology at the university, wishing she had an aptitude for physics or mathematics. It seemed to her a higher level of brain power was needed to do them, a level she could not hope to attain. They were the "real" sciences.

Rita Levi-Montalcini at Washington University in St. Louis, 1977. Rita moved to the United States after World War II, having survived persecution as a Jew and the terrible suffering of wartorn Italy.

In the summer of 1946 a letter arrived from Washington University in St. Louis; it came from the head of the zoology department there, a Viktor Hamburger, the same man whose paper inspired Rita's work on chick embryos. He had read the paper she wrote with Giuseppi Levi, and was inviting her to spend a semester in St. Louis so that they could investigate the problem together.

Levi urged her to accept; her mother did the same. Why not, then? Some of the old longing for adventure sprang up again, and that September Rita sailed from Genoa. A photograph taken aboard ship shows her smiling, wearing a short-skirted halter dress in a bright print, and enjoying the sunshine—a thin, elegant woman with slender ankles and black Italian sandals on her slender feet.

The ship docked at New York. "I felt at home the day I landed," she said, "there was great cordiality, generosity." She spent a few days with relatives, then went on to St. Louis and Viktor Hamburger—a German-born Jew who had fled from Hitler. She realized with joy that she had come to the right place and the right person, a man who was more than a distinguished scientist. He was, in her words, "a very sophisticated person . . . a very learned, very refined human being."

According to a fellow scientist, Hamburger was "the founding father of experimental neurobiology, and personally wonderful. To spend a day with Viktor is like being with the guru. He has such a wonderful humanity."

Rita kept her doubts about embryology and her own future to herself, and became acquainted with St. Louis. On campus, college girls knitted during lectures, which she could not understand. Black people were poor, they lived in wretched slums and were treated as inferiors, and this made her uncomfortable. In those days before the civil rights movement, blacks and whites inhabited separate worlds, so while America was generous and cordial, it was also less than perfect.

On Sundays she went to Bloomington, Indiana, to visit two old friends from medical school. They were in molecular biology and microbiology now, and they were "real" scientists, who had studied physics. One day she met James Watson, then twenty years old; with Francis Crick, a physicist, he was later to uncover the secrets of DNA and the double helix, in which the genetic code is embedded. Watson "had the appearance of an adolescent . . . absorbed and dreamy. . . . He took no interest in me whatsoever . . . an attitude I saw as part of his well-known antifeminism. I was never troubled by it."

A number of former physicists were turning to molecular biology. They, the physicists, meant to solve the problems of consciousness according to physical laws, but Levi-Montalcini had only her biologist's training. Even her old friends agreed there wasn't much future in what she was doing.

Depressed and sleeping badly, she went back to her laboratory and the experiment that had brought her there—the effects of amputation on developing nerve centers in chick embryos. In time Viktor saw what she had seen in the secret laboratory in Turin, and came to agree with her conclusion about the trophic factor. He was in fact so pleased with her work that he asked her to stay on. Her mother said she was by all means to stay on so long as she came home every summer for a month or so. But the depression continued, flaring up painfully whenever she went to Bloomington.

One day in January 1950 Viktor showed her a letter from a former student of his, Elmer Bueker, now living in New York. A recent paper of Bueker's explained work he'd been doing, work that seemed more interesting to Levi-Montalcini than it did to the author.

Instead of grafting extra limb buds onto chick embryos, as Hamburger had done, Elmer Bueker grafted tissues from cancerous tumors in mice. The tumors he chose grew very rapidly. And two of them, so-called sarcomas, caused nerve fibers to spring out from the nearby ganglia. This led Bueker to conclude that the tumor produced conditions favorable to the growth of nerve cells. A larger area to spread out in, perhaps.

But Rita was immediately struck by what she felt to be a coded message, hidden somewhere within Bueker's work—a message "whose meaning it was up to us to discover." Although Bueker had done this work two years ago and abandoned it, she and Hamburger agreed they ought to stop what they were doing and repeat his experiments. They wrote to ask Bueker's permission, obtained it, and sent off for a boxful of albino mice carrying the malignant tumors. When they came they seemed untroubled by their ailments, their bright red eyes full of life and curiosity.

Several mice were then sacrificed to medical science, and bits of tumor tissue transplanted onto the side of three-day-old chick embryos. Within days Rita's microscope showed that the mass of tumor cells had filled up with bundles of nerve fibers. "These fiber bundles passed between the cells like rivulets of water flowing steadily over a bed of stones," and they were not connected with the cells; they sprang out of the nearby ganglia.

The experiments were repeated over the course of months until, on a day in autumn, Rita saw something "so extraordinary that I thought I might be hallucinating." Not only was the tumor mass invaded by a thick network of nerve fibers, but there were nerve fibers also visible among other organs, the spleen, thyroid, and liver. She wondered if the last batch of mouse tumors was in some way different from earlier ones. What she knew, with a sudden conviction that was like the parting of a curtain, was that the tumors released a fluid and diffusable substance that speeded up growth in the nerve cells.

In fear and trembling she examined dozens of other embryos grafted with cells from the two effective tumors, terrified each time that nothing would happen; rejoicing when she saw, once again, the "miracle" of the mysterious substance.

One morning a familiar voice came thundering down the hallway—Giuseppe Levi, on his first visit to the United States. Surely he, more than anyone, would appreciate what she'd discovered.

She gave him a brief report of the work so far, and begged him to look through the microscope. As he looked, the old imperious anger filled the room. It was nonsense, he said. She would ruin her reputation and his if she published this work because those weren't nerve fibers at all, they were connective fibers, as any fool could see.

"Please," she said, "go and look at Arizona, such a beautiful place," and she put him on a plane, and spent the next three days setting up a device that projected images appearing through the microscope onto paper placed alongside it. That way it would be clear they were nerves, not connective fibers.

Levi remained unconvinced. "Maybe," he said when he returned, "but I don't believe it. Nor will you ever succeed in convincing me that a tumor can change the way nerve fibers grow."

Other people would have to be convinced. But how? She remembered Levi's early work with "in vitro" tissue culture techniques. Suppose she took a glass dish and placed in it a nerve ganglion with the tumor nearby. If nerve fibers sprang out from the ganglion in the dish, surely no one would then doubt that a fluid, diffusable substance was at work.

She decided to go to Brazil where a friend of hers had a laboratory with an extensive "in vitro" culture unit. It was of course unfortunate that Levi could not agree with her, but Levi was Levi—"I didn't care a bit what he said, I cared about what was correct." Yet his anger had stung all the same, bringing back the long-gone days when the old lion filled her with terror, just as her father once had.

In late summer, 1952, she boarded a plane for Italy, visited with her family, and then left for Brazil. A box containing two little white mice that bore cells of the effective cancers, traveled with her in her coat pocket. Their bright eyes peered out through holes in the top of the box, and from time to time they took bites from the apple she had fitted in with them.

The work in Rio de Janeiro was the start of the most intense period of Levi-Montalcini's life, bringing moments of great exultation, and other moments when nothing seemed to make sense. She ignored what didn't make sense; later on, she came to believe that success in science doesn't come from superior brain power, or unusually hard work, rather from the willingness to minimize obstacles. Very clever people often avoid work with too many obstacles, she says. Sensing failure, they veer away from it, while those who are perhaps less bright, but more stubborn, may not even see the obstacles.

She believed so strongly in what she was doing that she was willing to overlook failure and move on, disregarding negative information, trying new methods of attack. During those first few months, for example, her letters to Viktor in St. Louis reported a complete lack of success; bits of tumor tissue from one of the two little mice failed to bring about the luxuriant outgrowth of nerve fibers. Why? Perhaps a toxic factor of some kind was at work. Perhaps the toxic factor did not exist in tumors grown in their natural, mouse-tissue environment.

"I had only one card left to play and rested all my hopes upon it. . . ." She would transplant tumor cells from tumors that had previously been grafted onto chick embryos. There was no reason to believe it would work, yet in her heart of hearts she was convinced it would work.

Her reward was a dense halo of nerve fibers that sprang out from the ganglion in the dish, like the rays of a brilliant sun. She made drawings of them and sent them back to Viktor. She then repeated her experiment, and drew more of her beautiful halos, which enchanted her. Such was her enthusiasm that "I felt as if I too was a carrier of the tumor and subject to its prodigious effect," the marvelous halo springing out of her brain.

During the months in Rio she encountered other enigmas that troubled and sometimes shocked her, and they too had to be pushed aside for the time being. "The tumor effect exists!" as she wrote to Viktor, and that was what mattered. Overlooking all negative findings, she was resolved to spend her last month in Brazil exploring Rio. "Carnival was just about to begin, and the street resounded with the sounds of singing."

_____

Upon her return to the States Rita was met at the airport by Viktor with wonderful news—he had taken on a young biochemist, Stanley Cohen, to work with her in identifying the mysterious substance released by the tumors.

Stanley Cohen—Stan, as they called him from the start—proved to be totally different from people she'd worked with before, men like Levi, Hamburger, her friends and colleagues at medical school. The son of a Russian-born tailor, he'd gone to James Madison High in Brooklyn, then

Brooklyn College, then the University of Michigan. He wore a miscellaneous collection of clothing, limped slightly from childhood polio, and owned a mongrel dog that never left his side. Modest and somewhat reserved, Stan spoke like a Brooklyn boy, with a Brooklyn accent and vocabulary.

Rita was European to her fingertips, always carefully dressed and groomed, interested in the arts, elegant by nature and upbringing. Invitations to her dinner parties were sought after, because of her exquisite cooking, as well as the lively conversation in several languages. He was down-to-earth, she was an aristocrat. Yet as workmates the two fitted together so well that Stan told her once, "Rita, you and I are good, but together we are wonderful," and she never forgot those words; they surprised and flattered her.

Now her first task was to provide him with enough extract from the tumors so that he could find out what the substance was. This meant a year devoted to removing cancer tissues from dozens of chick embryos, a year of boring, unpleasant work on Rita's part. But it was the only way they could reach their goal, the analysis of the extract, which was Stan's task.

At the end of the year he announced it was a protein. Much more had to be known about this protein, but meanwhile papers were written and sent to scientific journals. Rita doubted that anybody read those papers. They were only accepted, she says now, because they carried Viktor Hamburger's name, as head of the department, along with hers and Stan's. And no one had ever heard of her or Stan. In fact, nobody took what they were doing seriously, which Stan believed to be a very good thing. When others took you seriously, he said, they buckled down to duplicating your work, then rushed ahead to develop it further. And "others" had big laboratories with expensive equipment, while they had only the two of them, give or take a couple of postdoctoral students to help out.

Stanley Cohen was never a believer in "big science." He enjoyed doing the work himself and getting calluses on his hands, and didn't mind that the "bright guys" paid no attention.

In succeeding years two other important sources of the substance they had come to call Nerve Growth Factor—NGF—were discovered: snake venom and the salivary glands of male mice. Stan also produced a specific antiserum to NGF, developed from the antidote for snakebite. He went on to discover another growth factor—EGF, for Epidermal Growth Factor. With each new discovery he said they had now used up all their luck, but the luck held out until 1958.

In December of that year Rita heard news "that for me sounded like the tolling of a funeral bell. . . ." Budget restrictions at Washington University prevented Viktor from offering Stan a permanent position. The following summer Stan left for another post, limping, his dog at his side, while Rita watched at the window, "thinking back with gratitude on the years spent together and looking forward with anxiety to those I would have to face without his precious aid."

The years ahead were not good ones, although for reasons she had not foreseen. She had the help of another biochemist, a talented young Italian, and the scientific world was becoming interested in Nerve Growth Factor. The trouble was that people repeated her experiments without mentioning how NGF was discovered. She came to conferences on the subject, and no one seemed to know she was there.

"My name was entirely left out of the literature. . . . I am

Dr. Levi-Montalcini working at her chosen profession in the research institute she set up in Rome.

not a person to be bitter, but it was astonishing to find it completely canceled." At the end of the 1960s she simply threw up her hands. "If they want NGF, I thought, they can have it," and she turned to work on the nerve cells of insects, dividing her time between St. Louis and Rome, where she established a small research institute. "I greatly enjoyed this beautiful work, but it had nothing to do with NGF. I did it just to get rid of this feeling of unhappiness at being completely ignored. . . ." During these years of being ignored, she developed a reputation as a fighter. "She has crossed swords at one time or another with everyone in this field," according to a colleague. Even Italy was not especially eager to have her. Scientists there were interested only in physics and molecular biology, and when she returned part-time, in 1962, she was snubbed and brushed aside.

By 1972 she had decided she could not give up her child, the Nerve Growth Factor, and went back to it again. Whether or not people gave her the credit didn't matter. It was her life's work, and she had no right to abandon it.

Then, in 1986 Nobel Prize for medicine was awarded to Stanley Cohen and Rita Levi-Montalcini. It was the end of her being ignored.

Today research on NGF is carried on in laboratories throughout the world. It is believed to hold clues to the fundamental nature of cancer, to Alzheimer's, Parkinson's, and Huntington's disease. EGF—Epidermal Growth Factor—is used in the treatment of severe burns. One day growth factors may unravel the central mystery of all biology, the process by which the single fertilized egg turns into a complex organism made up of billions of cells.

Rita Levi-Montalcini lives and works year-round in Italy now, where she is consulted unofficially by the Italian president and prime minister. "I had dinner with Gorbachev twice," she says, "he was wonderful to me." Schoolchildren come to see her, bringing gifts. Harvard offered her an honorary degree; she has declined many honorary degrees, "but you don't refuse Harvard." In her office she has put up a poster of Martin Luther King, Jr., whose civil rights work she admires, to remind her of her other home—she is a citizen of both countries, the United States and Italy. It was the family that drew her back, her longing to be with people of her own blood—her mother, who has since died, and her twin sister, Paola.

The sisters share an apartment in Rome, where Paola's steel and copper engravings enhance the walls; they have a massive, architectural quality. The furniture in this apartment is sleek, contemporary, all gleaming dark granite surfaces and black leather. But there is also a forest of green plants, cut flowers in vases—gladiolas, clouds of white daisies, irises and baby's breath—and more plants outside on the terrace. From this terrace can be seen the treetops of the Villa Torlonia, where Mussolini once lived.

It is not the kind of setting most women of eighty would choose, but Levi-Montalcini is an exceptional eighty-year-old. Still slim, straightbacked, and elegant, she wears heels and patterned sheer stockings, her hair piled in waves on top of her small head. She travels frequently to New York, Paris, and London. She searches out talent in the sciences and supports it; every young person who gets in touch with her finds her cordial, welcoming.

Paola, of whom she is intensely proud, has never married. She is one of Italy's foremost women artists. Giuseppe Levi lived into his eighties; his daughter Natalia became a world-famous writer. Viktor Hamburger is alive at almost ninety. Guido Boni became a physician in Turin. And Stan, Stanley Cohen, remains as modest as ever in spite of the Nobel, but is considerably better dressed than before.

Levi-Montalcini says, "the best of life is friendship. . . . It is very dangerous, especially for young people, to live in a state of obsession, always worried about career or success . . . we must keep our minds open to the problems of the larger society. . . ." And she continues to work. Work is her lifeblood. "The moment you stop working you are dead."

She doesn't work for the sake of mankind, she says, but for her own sake, just as she did fifty years ago before the great discoveries were made. She is still making discoveries. "It is a very attractive way to spend your time."

AFTERWORD

In the course of Nobel Week, Rosalyn Yalow gave a speech that took an unexpected approach. Instead of discussing science, she talked about women: "We still live in a world in which a significant fraction of people, including women, believe that a woman belongs and wants to belong exclusively in the home; that a woman should not aspire to achieve more than her male counterparts and particularly not more than her husband. Even now women with exceptional qualities . . . sense from their parents, teachers and peers that they must be harder-working, accomplish more and yet are less likely to receive appropriate rewards than are men. These are real problems which may never disappear. . . ."

There have been changes in the thirteen years since Rosalyn Yalow wrote those words, but the percentage of women choosing science as a career is hardly greater now than it was in the 1970s. Those women who do go into science stay away from the traditionally "masculine" fields, earning only 8 percent of the Ph.Ds in physics, for example, and 14 percent in computer sciences. Even in the life sciences the figure is only 35 percent. And whatever scientific field they enter, women tend to make their careers in teaching rather than research. They are less likely to fight for tenure, far less likely to become heads of departments.

Some people concerned with science education believe this may be due to certain characteristics of women, to their being less self-confident than men, less combative, less eager to tear others down in order to win an argument. In short, they believe that most women prefer cooperation to competition.

Looking back at the lives of the four women Nobel laureates, there is certainly evidence for such a belief. Maria Mayer, for example, put off publishing the theory that eventually won her Nobel Prize, out of modesty and a lack of fighting spirit. Rita Levi-Montalcini thought of herself as intellectually inferior because she could never master physics. Even Rosalyn Yalow, who claims to be "a tough baby," was willing to take second place in public to her working partner, a man she admired, but labeled "a male chauvinist pig." And Barbara McClintock retreated into silent isolation when fellow scientists ignored her revolutionary discoveries.

But if little has changed since the seventies, there is good reason to anticipate change in the future. In the years to come a greater percentage of scientists will be women, because there will be fewer men available. This is simply a matter of demographics, statistics related to population. "The number of white males of college age . . . is predicted to drop significantly in the future," according to Sheila E. Widnall, a professor of Aeronautics at MIT. Women and minorities, she says, will have to take up the slack.

Today the American science establishment is beating the bushes in search of women and members of ethnic minorities. There has never been a better time for those who were formerly barred from the exclusive club that was science.

It may well be that ways of doing scientific research will change in the process, that competition will give way to cooperation as women take their rightful place in the laboratories. Perhaps we can even look forward to a time when half the Nobel Prizes will be won by women.

However, it is well to remember that the prizes and honors go only to a very few. For most scientists of either sex, seeing what no one else has ever seen before—even without winning major awards for the discovery—is the true reward. Like music, painting, and poetry, science gives pleasure to those willing to learn its mysteries, and the pleasure endures for a lifetime.

WOMEN NOBEL LAUREATES
IN SCIENCE

Marie Curie	1903	Physics
Marie Curie	1911	Chemistry
Irene Joliot-Curie*	1935	Chemistry
Gerty Cori	1947	Medicine
Maria Goeppert-Mayer	1963	Physics
Dorothy Hodgkin	1964	Chemistry
Rosalyn Yalow	1977	Medicine
Barbara McClintock	1983	Medicine
Rita Levi-Montalcini	1986	Medicine
Gertrude Elion	1988	Medicine

Marie Curie's daughter.

——————— BIBLIOGRAPHY ———————

FOREWORD

Wilhelm, Peter. *The Nobel Prize*. London: Springwood Books, 1983.

MARIA GOEPPERT-MAYER

Dash, Joan. *A Life of One's Own: Three Gifted Women and the Men They Married*. New York: Harper & Row, 1973.

Dash, Joan. Telephone conversation with Maria Wentzel, December 1989.

Dash, Joan. Telephone conversation with Robert G. Sachs, December 1989.

Goeppert-Mayer, Maria, Papers. Central University Library, University of California, San Diego.

Hall, Mary Harrington. "The Nobel Genius." *San Diego Magazine*, August 1964, p. 64.

Rhodes, Richard. *The Making of the Atomic Bomb,* New York: Simon & Schuster, 1986.

Sachs, Robert G. *Maria Goeppert-Mayer, 1906–1972, A Biographical Memoir*. Washington, D.C.: The National Academy of Science of the United States, 1979.

ROSALYN YALOW

Kahn, Carol. "She Cooks, She Cleans, She Wins the Nobel Prize." *Family Health,* June 1978, p.24.

Keerdoja, Eileen, and Slate, William "A Nobel Woman's Hectic Pace," *Newsweek,* October 29, 1979, p. 21.

Kent, L. "Winner Woman." *Vogue,* January 1978, p. 131.

Les Prix Nobel en 1977. Stockholm: The Nobel Foundation, 1978.

Overbye, Dennis. "Rosalyn Yalow: Lady Laureate of the Bronx." *Discover,* June 1982, p. 40.

People, January 2, 1978. No author given. "A Nobel Laureate from the Bronx Gives Medicine its Most Sensitive Chemical Detector." p. 95.

Stone, Elizabeth. "Mme. Curie from the Bronx." *The New York Times Magazine,* April 9, 1978, p. 29.

Yalow, Rosalyn. Interview by Joan Dash. New York, July 1989.

Yalow, Rosalyn. "What's Ahead for Women in Medicine." *Parents,* January 1978, p. 38.

BARBARA McCLINTOCK

Campbell, Allan M. Letter to author, September 1989.

Clark, Matt, and Shapiro, Dan. "The Kernel of Genetics." *Newsweek,* November 30, 1981, p. 74.

Creighton, Harriet. Letter to author, December 1989.

Dash, Joan. Telephone conversation with Ernest Sears, December 1989.

Dash, Joan. Telephone conversation with Bruce Wallace, July 1989.

Gould, Stephen Jay. "Triumph of a Naturalist." *The New York Review of Books,* March 29, 1984, p. 3.

Judson, Horace Freeland. *The Eighth Day of Creation: Makers of the Revolution in Biology.* New York: Simon & Schuster, 1979.

Keller, Evelyn Fox. *A Feeling for the Organism: The Life and Work of Barbara McClintock.* San Francisco: W. H. Freeman, 1983.

Les Prix Nobel en 1983. Stockholm: The Nobel Foundation, 1984.

Shine, Ian, and Wrobel, Sylvia. *Thomas Hunt Morgan: Pioneer of Genetics.* Lexington: University Press of Kentucky, 1976.

Stadler, David. Interview by Joan Dash. Seattle, July 1989.

Wilcox, Fred. "Everyone Suddenly Pays Honor to a Geneticist Most Persistent." *Cornell Alumni News,* February 1982, p. 2.

RITA LEVI-MONTALCINI

Ginzburg, Natalia. *All Our Yesterdays.* Carcenet, Manchester, England: 1956.

Ginzburg, Natalia. *Family Sayings.* New York: Dutton, 1967.

Levi-Montalcini, Rita. *In Praise of Imperfection: My Life and Work.* New York: Basic Books, 1988.

Levi-Montalcini, Rita. Interview by Joan Dash. Rome, April 1989.

Levi, Primo. *Periodic Table.* New York: Schocken, 1984.

Liversidge, Anthony. "Interview with Rita Levi-Montalcini." *Omni.* March, 1988, p. 70.

Pedemonte, Enrico. "Lo Spettacolo Nucleare." *L'Espresso.* April 1989, p. 192.

Randall, Frederika. "The Heart and Mind of a Genius." *Vogue,* March 1987, p. 480.

Marx, Jean L. "The 1986 Nobel Prize for Physiology or Medicine." *Science,* October 31, 1986, p. 543.

AFTERWORD

Widnall, Sheila E. "AAAS Presidential Lecture: Voices from the Pipeline." *Science,* September 30, 1988, p. 1740.

INDEX

M

N

O

P

——— ABOUT THE AUTHOR ———

J oan Dash grew up in Brooklyn, graduated from Barnard
College, and then went with her husband, a physicist,
to Los Alamos, New Mexico, the town where the atomic
bomb was born. Her first book, "A Life of One's Own: Three
Gifted Women and the Men They Married," included a pro-
file of Maria Goeppert-Mayer, who won the Nobel Prize for
work in theoretical physics. This in turn inspired an interest
in women scientists, their motivations, and the hardships
they encounter in pursuing careers in what has been until
recently a male stronghold.

Dash's next book was "Summoned to Jerusalem: The
Life of Henrietta Szold." She has written many short stories,
including a number for "Seventeen," and is currently at
work on "Disturbing the Peace," a book for young adults on
the subject of social activism.

Photo Acknowledgments

AP/Wide World Photos: pp. 84, 96; Copyright © The Nobel Foundation: p. xiv, 34, 66,
98; Courtesy of the Archives, California Institute of Technology: p. 93; Courtesy of
Dr. Rita Levi-Montalcini: p. 119; Courtesy of the University of California, San Diego: p.
14; Courtesy of Maria Wentzel: p. 30; Courtesy of Dr. Rosalyn S. Yalow: p. 63;
Georgianna Silk/ © 1982 Discover Publications: pp. 45, 61; Massimo Vergari; courtesy of
Dr. Rita Levi-Montalcini: p. 128.